AFTER COETZEE

AFTER COETZEE

AN ANTHOLOGY OF ANIMAL FICTIONS

Edited by A. Marie Houser

FAUNARY PRESS
Minneapolis, MN 55401
www.faunarypress.com

Copyright © 2017 by A. Marie Houser
Copyright of individual works is maintained by the respective writers.

All rights reserved. No part of this book may be reproduced without written permission from the publisher, except in the case of brief quotations for use in critical articles and reviews.

"Encomium: Sun" by Gabriel Gudding first appeared in *Literature for Nonhumans* (Ahsahta Press, 2015), and is reprinted by permission of the author and Ahsahta Press. "A Blinded Horse Dreams of Hippocampi" by Justin Maxwell first appeared in *Eleven Eleven*, Issue 19, 2015 and *A Blinded Horse Dreams of Hippocampi & Other Plays* (Alligator Pear Publishing, 2016), and is reprinted by permission of the author and Alligator Pear Publishing. "Our Fathers, Which Aren't in Heaven" by W.P. Osborn first appeared in *Seven Tales and Seven Stories* (Unboxed Books, 2013), and is reprinted by permission of the author. "Galaxies Beyond Violet" by Melanie Rae Thon first appeared in *Five Points*, Vol. 15, Nos. 1 and 2, 2012, and is reprinted by permission of the author. "How to Kill Butterflies" by Laura Madeline Wiseman first appeared in *Grasslands Review*, Issue 27, 2008, and is reprinted by permission of the author.

Cover image: Kathryn Eddy, *Plastic Animals Can't Scream*, digital print, 2010.
Used by permission.

Publisher's Cataloging-in-Publication data
Names: Houser, A. Marie, editor.
Title: After Coetzee : an anthology of animal fictions / edited by A. Marie Houser.
Description: Includes bibliographical references. | Minneapolis, MN: Faunary Press, 2017.
Identifiers: ISBN 978-0-9966245-1-0 (pbk.) | 978-0-9966245-0-3 (Kindle) | 978-0-9966245-2-7 (epub) | LCCN 2017940391
Subjects: LCSH Animals—Fiction. | Human-animal relationships—Fiction. | Animal rights—Moral and ethical aspects—Fiction. | Literature—Collections. | Poetry. | Short stories. | BISAC LITERARY COLLECTIONS / General
Classification: LCC PS648.A5 A38 2017 | DDC 808.83/936—dc23

Printed in the United States of America
First printing, 2017

2 4 6 8 10 9 7 5 3

For the billions who speak but go unheard.

CONTENTS

INTRODUCTION ... ix
A. Marie Houser

NOTES ... xxvii

NUMBER 2 PENCILS FOR THE WHITE CAT ... 3
Kyoko Yoshida

OUR FATHERS, WHICH AREN'T IN HEAVEN ... 7
W.P. Osborn

THE GOAT ... 29
David Brooks

WHO IS THIS DIMAGGIO? ... 43
J.T. Townley

PROCYON LOTOR ... 57
Ariana-Sophia Kartsonis

RED ADMIRAL ... 61
Jonathan Balcombe

ONE OF YOUR NUMBER ... 69
Diane Josefowicz

A BLINDED HORSE DREAMS OF HIPPOCAMPI *Justin Maxwell*	*85*
CURES AND SUPERSTITIONS *Michael X. Wang*	*95*
GALAXIES BEYOND VIOLET *Melanie Rae Thon*	*117*
ENCOMIUM: SUN *Gabriel Gudding*	*129*
HER MAN *Amy Cicchino*	*141*
HOW TO KILL BUTTERFLIES *Laura Madeline Wiseman*	*145*
TRUTH BE TOLD *David Armstrong*	*155*
THE END OF THE LINE *Olga Kotnowska*	*167*
THE SKY ABOVE CHAIRS *Gary Barwin*	*179*
ABOUT THE CONTRIBUTORS	*181*
ABOUT THE EDITOR	*187*
ACKNOWLEDGMENTS	*189*

INTRODUCTION

A. Marie Houser

"Derrida suggests that it is both ethically and philosophically appropriate to follow, or come after."
—Lynn Turner, *The Animal Question in Deconstruction*

"A little bird follows Theseus into the labyrinth gobbling down the thread..."
—J.M. Coetzee, "Samuel Beckett and the Temptations of Style," *Doubling the Point: Essays and Interviews*

Why so much dog? the instructor asked in workshop. And here dog had seemed an uncontroversial choice for my story's deuteragonist: I could have chosen a coelacanth, a calf, a gibbon. Or made the dog a protagonist. I had found myself less interested in "workshop realism," which after all concerned itself so narrowly with human desire and need. But I didn't say so. As a student those years ago, I resembled a surprised bird more than a young woman; my tongue could not answer.

Dogs have been our shadow and our concern for thousands of years—or we, theirs. The most obvious rejoinder, then, is this: nonhuman animals exist. "I speak to you of frogs," the eponymous protagonist of J.M. Coetzee's *Elizabeth*

Costello announces. "Of frogs and of my belief or beliefs and of the relation between the former and the latter. Because they exist."[1]

Nonhuman worlds overlap, withdraw from, and overtake our own; they are our own. Dogs, of course, share our homes, but we are also mobile pillars of bacteria. Subterranean nematodes live miles deep within the earth, far from human ken; automobiles stop as goslings cross the road. Societies of cockroaches, waiting out daylight, breathe like accordions through the bellows of their tracheoles.

But the view from our literature has been bipedal, non-ultraviolet; it is often—quite literally—a *view*. We have taken sight to be the rhetorical locus of perception and cognition,[2] and so employ it as our chief sense in mainstream literature. Our texts don't often follow a scent as dogs would or seek a phenomenology of touch the way octopuses do. Or know a thing by the heat it generates, as the rattlesnake in Melanie Rae Thon's gorgeous "Galaxies Beyond Violet" in this anthology does. Having "no wish to harm or strike," the rattlesnake perceives a woman in the desert as "warm waves wafting into pits on his face, opening ion channels, triggering nerves to the optic tectum where vision refines heat to form a shivery field of radiant colors, an infrared thermal image: gold and orange, rimmed with turquoise." In Thon's galaxies, a snake is an animal beside another animal, rather than the serpent of theology, and the apotheosis of love is the honeybee: "I make myself in her image. ... So lovingly she lands!" A literature without *dog*—a literature without *snake* and *bee*—means a whole bright (and scented) spectrum of stories is missing.[3]

Why so much dog? Today I'd reply, "J.M. Coetzee. *Disgrace*." I would describe the shift in David Lurie, the novel's protagonist, from debased aesthete to a man who discovers moral salvage, if not salvation, through communion with dogs condemned to death. But we didn't study a literature that concerned itself with nonhuman animals. Coetzee's thematic triptych *Disgrace*, *The Lives of Animals*, and *Elizabeth Costello* had only recently appeared—ahead of the nonhuman-animal turn that would amplify their concerns. Arguably, they presaged that turn, giving full expression to themes that had skittered on the edge of academic and writing communities, yawing between their hostility and indifference.[4]

To writers of a certain conscience, Coetzee's triptych provided an opening, indeed gave permission, to seriously address our misapprehension of nonhuman animals, question our figurations of them, and engage them in our texts as subjects in themselves, for themselves. Once verboten in mainstream literature, the concerns and prerogatives of nonhuman animals, and of the humans challenged to understand them, are now generating lively, innovative, and ethically charged works. Those works are collected in *After Coetzee: An Anthology of Animal Fictions*. Contributed by Jonathan Balcombe, Gary Barwin, Gabriel Gudding, Diane Josefowicz, Justin Maxwell, Melanie Rae Thon, Laura Madeline Wiseman, and other talented writers, they honor, follow, and succeed at the task Coetzee set forth in the three books: to think, and write, animals.

How to think and write (literature) about animals is a question situated in a particular historical moment. Enlightenment thought had been under a gathering storm of suspicion for more than a century, fomented by anti-colonialism and anti-imperialism. This suspicion sharpened into a repeated critique: Western philosophical and socio-political systems had essentialized the white, able-bodied, bourgeoisie male into an idea of the universal human subject and operated violently on its behalf. The universal human subject was supposed to be autonomous and rational, tilting toward progress and perfectibility, and therefore exceptional among animal life.

Yet despite crucial analyses by black radical thinkers, postcolonial theorists, and ecofeminists,[5] the very effort to construct "the human" above and against "the animal" has received critical focus only in the last decade and a half. Key developments in the early 2000s announced the nonhuman-animal turn: a posthumanism concerned with metaphysical anthropocentrism emerged,[6] while animal studies became politicized and the field of critical animal studies was defined.[7]

At a crucial moment just prior, in 1999, J.M. Coetzee published *Disgrace* and *The Lives of Animals*. As novels, the works uniquely foreground that *thinking* animals is indelibly braided with *writing* animals.[8] While *Disgrace* thematizes the violent legacies of the Western intellectual tradition for humans and nonhumans both, *The Lives of Animals* anticipates the next decade's focus on nonhuman animals in its protagonist Elizabeth Costello, a kind of ur-animal-studies-scholar, alone in her ethical approach but convinced of its rightness.

Disgrace follows David Lurie, a white English professor in post-Apartheid South Africa. Lurie is a Romanticist who commits a "not quite" rape of a student and is called to account at a disciplinary hearing.[9] He exiles himself afterward to his daughter's rural smallholding, where the Luries endure humiliation and trauma. As a kind of personal and historical expatiation, Lurie volunteers at a vet clinic, holding dogs through euthanasia and caring for their bodies after death. Slowly he relinquishes the aesthetic egoism that had subsumed the reality of other lives, other sufferings. Inspired by Driepoot, a favored dog he will give up to death, he thinks to pen a "singing…or howling…lament" into his opera.[10]

But Lurie does not develop this zoopoetic opera—"probably mercifully," one critic writes.[11] Yet its incompleteness means that, with no "lament"[12] to taint the "Lösung" of euthanasia, the disposability of dogs remains an unwritten, unrecorded "blank."[13] Lurie instead disappears into the role of "psychopomp,"[14] oriented toward death and the immortal, longing to write one transcendent note but letting the idea dissipate in his imagination, where failure cannot reach art. Perfectionism is at the heart of human-centered conceptions of value: aesthetic, but also ethical. Perhaps we need the unmerciful music of a baying canine and a plinky banjo.[15]

Elizabeth Costello, contra Lurie, is oriented to art and to "the lives of animals," and so, in editing this book, I looked to the restless agnosticism, the radical openness, that Costello represents. My use of "agnosticism" refers to theorist Matthew Calarco's efforts to articulate an expansive ethics, one that surpasses the usual niggling questions about who and what "deserves" moral considerability.[16] This ethics is comprised of an encounter between other and self in which the other calls upon the self to alleviate the other's suffering.

Calarco names this ethics of the encounter "generously *agnostic*" because it does not demarcate the ways that encounter might occur or what sort of being the other shows up as.[17]

The Costello novels suggest that literature can constitute an encounter.[18] Costello herself wants a poetry "that does not try to find an idea in an animal, that is not about the animal, but is instead a record of engagement with him."[19]

In *The Lives of Animals,* Costello, an eminent novelist, delivers two lectures for a college's annual speaker series. In them, she argues that the epistemologies of philosophy, science, and theology are threaded through with anthropocentrism and have therefore thoroughly and violently misapprehended nonhuman animals. Instead of the rupturing discourses they have produced, she would have a bodily sympathy of the sort that can be communicated through the language of poetry. Costello's esteem for poetry may perplex; after all, she is a novelist. But her primary concern is less with genre than with "how to bring the living body into being within ourselves."[20]

Costello's lectures themselves constitute a response to the encounter as fiction and nonfiction—to the "mute appeal"[21] of Red Peter, the ape-cum-scholar in Kafka's "Report to an Academy," and to that of Sultan, the captive chimpanzee who features in psychologist Wolfgang Köhler's *The Mentality of Apes.* On stage, Costello is "take[n] over," speaking with and as Red Peter, and, through him, with and as Sultan. "He"—a double he—"is us," as she says in another context.[22]

In 2003, Coetzee gathered the two chapters that comprise *The Lives of the Animals* together with six new chapters to form *Elizabeth Costello.* The additional chapters deepen our understanding of Costello: she asserts—she may even reassert—but she also self-contradicts.[23] She does so out of an intellectual humility, no matter her occasionally imperious tone, and a suspicion that self-certainty, viz., Cartesian self-certainty, authorizes conceptual and physical violence toward nonhuman animals. So while Costello would counter reductionist discourses with poetry, she thinks she has in no way settled the question of making literature responsible to the more-than-human. Representation of nonhuman animals remains a "Rubik cube" for Costello, as she calls understanding in general, yet to be solved—and perhaps is unsolvable.[24]

After Coetzee: An Anthology of Animal Fictions is an experiment in agnosticism. Taken together, the contributions approach puzzle-solving with a range of styles, registers, genres, and generic inventions. Mostly consisting of short fiction—or fictions, to emphasize the point about insolvability—they are primarily realist, but also comprise the horrific, the comedic, and the fabulist. And in answer to Costello, who calls on poetry to counter reductionist discourses, the contributions also include prose-poem texts by Gary Barwin and Gabriel Gudding and a lyrical monologue by playwright Justin Maxwell.

Agnosticism was my watchword not only for genre and style, but also content. I had interest in representing a range of beings, from *so much dog* to snakes, calves, fishes, and honeybees, open to whichever might show up in the contributions and to however they might show up—as protagonists, as subjects, or as otherwise. My hope was that, by representing multiplicity, the anthology would not be taken to represent "animality," or "the animal," phantom categories into which all nonhuman beings have been consigned.[25]

Kyoko Yoshida's "Number 2 Pencils for the White Cat," the anthology opener, addresses the anxiety of representation. (Spoilers ahead.) The eponymous cat of Yoshida's story visits a Mr. Crow at his window. The visits are as inscrutable as they are recursive: what does the cat hope to find? We don't know. The cat relays a story to Mr. Crow, but the narrator omits it "for editorial purposes." And though Mr. Crow mines the story to produce a bestseller, he remains insensible to its potential to illumine the cat and those return visits. The cat's near incomprehensibility is owing not to the cat's "animality," then, but to anthropocentric assumptions about literature. The narrator regards the cat's story as expendable, and so omits it; Mr. Crow regards the story as not really belonging to the cat and so takes it.[26]

I have thoroughly spoiled Yoshida's piece because, as the opener, it brings the reader into dialogue with the anthology at the outset. Though most pieces do not invite or require the heightened critical response Yoshida's does, they invite curiosity, openness, and attunement. Yoshida's piece also sets a distinct tone for other pieces to amplify, riff away from, or respond to contrapuntally.

Many of the contributions seek a different tonal nuance and depth—moments of gorgeous awe and twittering levity as well as pathos—and find it in surprising ways. The delight of W.P. Osborn's "Our Fathers, Which Aren't in Heaven," to which we turn shortly, is in the narrator's fusty, high-toned register, incongruent against the chaos of the zoo. In contrast, Gary Barwin's "The Sky Above Chairs" is a wondrous, otherworldly meditation on our mystification of animals. Metaphor floats on metaphor—beginning with "chairs," a stand-in for "animals"—in a sublime of misrecognition. So "we" observe: "They waited as one, then leapt the fence in a single thought, a flock of birds, their wings silent and invisible." As the anthology's closer, Barwin's piece echoes our opening themes.

Occasionally, I would disagree with a line, only to find the story's overarching ethos win out.[27] The narrator in David Armstrong's "Truth Be Told" does not think that the deer in the story could have "known herself," for instance as a sexed or gendered being (she thinks of herself as "it"). The deer, to that narrator's estimation, reacts rather than responds meaningfully. But for all their "intellectual re-appropriation of objects," the humans neither know themselves nor respond meaningfully. They think they do, but the heartbreaking final line gives other testament.

Some contributions follow after Costello by doing as she adjures poets to do: represent the "full being" of nonhuman animals. Several stage rescue, resistance, captivity, and compulsory dependence, and include surprising takes on "pets"—cats, as in the protagonist of J.T. Townley's "Who Is This DiMaggio?," and, of course, dogs. They seem to take seriously the double bind that Elizabeth Costello identifies: nonhuman animals are imagined as corporeal substance—flesh-and-hair planes of res extensa. Yet they are interred in spaces that confine those limbs, where being is most felt, in particular "the flow of joy that comes from … being an embodied-being."[28]

W.P. Osborn's hapless elephant in "Our Fathers, Which Aren't In Heaven" is one such being. Captured in hopes his albinism will draw crowds to a failing zoo, he is soon at the center of a hyper-bureaucracy. The zoo-management collective, of which the narrator is a part, maintains a polite and deliberative but completely unsound decision-making process. "It was thought well to publish...a booklet we could feature in the souvenir shop," the narrator remarks, "the proceeds to defray the wages of the calligraphers we hired..."

The elephant suffers and takes to banging his head. The narrator does not seem to recognize this stereotypy, or other stress behaviors, as such. As though subjection were enlistment, he calls pachyderms darted for fighting in too-close quarters "fallen comrades-in-arms." He also calls the elephant "the white," reflective of the racism behind the ostensible reason for the animal's capture: protection from the native population. But naming also becomes a route to sympathy for the elephant. A humorous conceit about what to finally name him, threaded through the piece, suggests that the narrator *can* honor the resistance of animal being to reductionism—though that doesn't much help the elephant in life.

Several contributions address naming as nomenclature, how we collapse the astonishing array of difference, and ablate the individual lives, within a species-set through classification and collection. Jonathan Balcombe's short story, the introspective "Red Admiral," describes a biologist's early enchantment with insects that was lamentably diverted into specimen collecting. Balcombe, an ethologist known for his game-changing books on nonhuman-animal sentience, such as *What a Fish Knows*, appears as a fiction writer for the first time here.

Diane Josefowicz's "One of Your Number" imagines the consequences of the taxonomist's work from the perspective of one who has been collected. The captive, a primate in a zoo, mimics nomenclature to lob complaints at those who made his seizure inevitable: "*H. taxonomicus*," the scientists, and "*H. economicus*," the developers who ruined his home "with their river-damming, clear-cutting, and, not least, fire-setting..." From the time of his capture to the story's present, he has been identified, misidentified, and entirely unseen as a singular being by zoo keepers. And so he declares: "Once my name was Bertram Outram, and I was not an orphan." *Once*, Outram says. But Bertram's statement of life, one that pointedly affirms both his relationality (he had parents) and his singularity (he had a name), contains the hope for its continuance: Bertram Outram is still "Bertram Outram," and he speaks.

This speaking is partially what turns the axis of genre. If a nonhuman-animal character speaks, we are accustomed to think, we must be inside a work of fabulism, fantasy, or children's literature: a speaking animal is anthropomorphic and therefore a touch too fantastic. (Yoshida's piece deftly plays with this assumption through troubling genre, creating a fable of fabulism itself.)

In literature, every line of dialogue, and every internal thought, is a facsimile and translation. The messiness of human speech is made comprehensible only through stylistic conventions, and the closer fictional dialogue is to real speech, the more parodic it sounds. Nonhuman-animal thought and communication is no less translatable—except to a parsimonious imagination. Jacques Derrida asks: in forbidding ourselves to "assign, interpret or project" meaning to/in another animal's gesture, gaze, or speech, aren't we "depriving the animal of every power of manifestation, of the desire to manifest *to me* anything at all, and even to manifest to me in some way *its* experience of *my* language, of *my* words and of *my* nudity?"[29]

When the narrator of Ariana-Sophia Kartsonis's "*Procyon lotor*" speaks of her "fabulous hands," I take that speaking seriously. I believe a raccoon would appreciate her own handiwork: not just in grasping and turning latches, but in helping another raccoon escape, even as she mourns "those fallen-us left behind." Her conjoining of "fallen" and "us" into "fallen-us" commixes being in mutuality and mortality; it manifests an "experience of language" that contrasts with our own, atomized, ways of speaking.

More-than-human worlds are fluttered through with communication, from the syntactical complexity of bird song to the waggle and sickle dances of bees. There also exists bodily rhetorics that constitute refusals to communicate with humans or indifference to doing so, and those meant for contact, such as a horse's pointing ears.[30] In Justin Maxwell's hallucinatory and mournful "A Blinded Horse Dreams of Hippocampi," the seahorses speak to the horse of "our song," and the horse replies:

> My withers tense,
> motion in my darkness,
> the screen of blindness,
> the songs calling me down
> into the depth of the sea.

Perhaps what we disavow when we refuse the speech of other animals are these uncanny sounds and songs of mourning, shared across species, as when Amy Cicchino's canine protagonist whimpers at "Her Man." Laura Madeline Wiseman's "How to Kill Butterflies" makes explicit the ways in which fear of feminizing associations drives our turning from, and violence against, other animals.[31] This time, a human girl is surrounded by brutalization, and rather than whimper, she muffles her distress under acts of insecticide—one of a few notes of violence towards nonhumans allowed into the anthology; violence towards humans is depicted in Michael Wang's "Cures and Superstitions."

Of course, a naïve literary anthropomorphism can work *against* other beings, remaking them in the image of "the human," that petit god. The contributions to this anthology offer models for resisting naïveté. For instance, Jonathan Balcombe, Diane Josefowicz, and Melanie Rae Thon ground their depictions in empirical detail, an approach that recalls ethologist Marc Bekoff's concept of "biocentric athropomorphism."[32] At the same time, their writerly "feel for [the animal's] experience" suggests the attunement to other bodies, their movements, that ecofeminists advocate.[33] Justin Maxwell and Gabriel Gudding, to whom I turn shortly, achieve distance through a Shklovskian defamiliarization, interpreted as poetic invention. (Shklovksy makes clear that fiction written from a nonhuman animal's perspective is also sufficient to shake up our somnolent automatisms.)[34]

But I am reminded of Coetzee's critical essay "Into the Dark Chamber: The Novelist and South Africa," which discusses a scene from Nadine Gordimer's *Burger's Daughter*: "What Rosa suffers and waits for is a time when humanity will be restored across the face of society, and therefore when all human acts, including the flogging of an animal, will be returned to the ambit of moral judgment."[35] Until such a time arrives, perhaps the more pressing concern is that, for fear of endorsing a naïve literary *anthropomorphism*, we succumb to a quiet literary *anthropocentrism*, one that shuts out other beings.

Though a decade had passed between the publication of *Elizabeth Costello* in 2003 and the first call for submissions for this project, writers would sometimes query for examples. A literature meant to take seriously that animals are beings with prerogatives and projects seemed fantastical. But after more than a year and a half, contributors thankfully came forward with pieces ready for this kind of anthology.

It's not widely known that prior to the Enlightenment, when human supremacism became focalized in a Cartesian conception of "Man"—uniquely rational, endlessly adaptive, and therefore language-producing—texts brimmed with nonhuman animals, who sometimes exerted preferences or thumped and honked out their own recalcitrance. Those bodies were there in the texts, and not merely as pre-Fordist conveyances of pelts, eggs, meat, gullets, oils, and innards, insensible to their own suffering. Michel de Montaigne writes in "An Apology for Raymond Sebond": "For why shall a gosling not say thus: 'All the parts of the universe have me in view: the earth serves for me to walk on, the sun to give me light, the stars to breathe their influences into me.... I am the darling of nature.'"[36]

Forward to the nineteenth century, when representations of nonhumans as worlding beings became representations of those beings as subjected and abused. Then, writers made a literary case for nonhuman animals: Leo Tolstoy, for instance, whose "Kholstomer" details the sufferings of a horse,[37] and Mark Twain, whose anti-vivisectionist "A Dog's Tale" is surely an answer to the question *why so much dog*.[38]

By the twentieth century, literature had come to treat nonhuman animals as supernumerary background players, transcendent tropes, and transitive objects to be acted upon. They were inert bodies that responded to stimuli or landed on the scene to illumine human drama. In fantasy literature, they appeared as therianthropic shapeshifters, and in children's literature, as fur-vehicles for moral messages that, with few exceptions, centered duties and obligations towards *humans*.[39] Other times, figurative animals received mention as consumables, hunted or "humanely" killed in back-to-the-land narratives.

In recent decades, the rank-and-file approach to the nonhuman animal has been the ranch-and-farm pastoral and the sacrificial sublime of primarily, but not exclusively, Western and Midwestern writers. They described the butchering of chickens and the parting of pastern from hoof as inevitable as the seasons: natural, dutiful, virtuous.[40]

Their literature followed the genealogy of axiological developments. Out of an *aesthetic appreciation of nature* in the eighteenth century emerged ethics, or right action concerning the *use of nature*. In the United States, Aldo Leopold's "land ethic" would manage, among other things, "a food chain aimed to harmonize the wild and the tame in the joint interest of stability, productivity, and beauty."[41] So the wide-focus view of the pastoral, which prized certain tableaux—the wooly geometrics of bison bent over a hill—was reflected in concern not for the suffering individual, but for the transorganic, unsuffering whole: species, ecosystems, the planet.

If animals were mourned, as "wild" or "feral" animals sometimes had been, they were mourned as synecdochic representatives for species threatened or devastated as part of a general environmental harm. I am aware of no such literature, for instance, that considers the perspective of a "meat animal," as the narrator of David Brooks's moving and sharply drawn short story "The Goat" does. The story's namesake, who languishes tethered and abandoned in a yard, moves the narrator to wonder how he would feel, "alone for all that time": "One day the woman there, and the dog, the cat, and the next all gone. No explanation."

The recent burst of popular and literary attention to nonhuman animals has made the question *why so much dog* moot in one way: somewhere around one-hundred fiction titles published in 2016 contain the word "dog."[42] We also find a renewed appreciation of "the wild" in our poetry and fiction, which has come to recognize the lifeworlds of other beings. But if there is now *so much* dog, there is not so much coelacanth, calf, gibbon, babirusa, gecko, goat, and pig—the eaten, the unfamiliar, the unlovely.[43]

This bibliopolitical regulation of the literary animal attends the biopolitical regulation of real-world animals. Whereas some dogs, cats, and other "petlike" animals are brought into our grace as honorary family members, so long as they make themselves amenable, billions of other animals are sequestered in laboratories, zoos, farms, and slaughterhouses: rabbits, cows, pigs, sheep, goats, rats, turkeys, chickens, chimpanzees, marmosets, and such a panoply of hoof-footed, scaled, or wing-wending beings. Animal bodies—animal lives—have become the indelible but unseen, unfelt mark on who "we" are: ghost flesh against our flesh, passing unnoticed through our pores, mouths, ears, lungs, families, cities. They are oozed into cosmetics and chemicals; they are broken down into food.

In his blistering prose-poem "Encomium: Sun," Gabriel Gudding writes that, as against what "[e]verybody knows," few understand the ways in which farms and slaughterhouses dissever the families and bodies of nonhuman animals: "the suckling motions of /calves, the access of the faces of calves to the /milk of the udders of the mothers the cows, /is managed, the access of lips of piglets to /the teats of pigs…is placed on a confederated schedule…"

Gudding fluidizes genre, disrupts it as he does sense and syntax, shaking them up so as to shake out our speciesisms, just the way that entire economies are built on supposedly fungible farmed-animal bodies, each a mini-meat factory. But by the end, portmanteaus erupt with a surplus of meaning, a seeding of joyful resistance, and the narrator may congratulate his "d[a[we]][la]ughter of / her fa(r)ther." Nonetheless, this joyful resistance is constrained by and conjoined with death: an encomium is a form of praise that may be delivered as a eulogy.

We must "be sad as in a zoo," as Gudding admonishes. But not for long. The water prisons of our aquariums are failing. The canvas wardens of our circuses have come undone. Our acts may yet be entering the "ambit of moral judgment."

And so I look to the future, when we may surpass the questions we have asked for hundreds of years—can animals think? speak? feel?—and *still* ask, only with more precision: Can chickens do well at math and are they sometimes wily and deceitful? Do nematodes who live in earth and ice compose messages from chemical lexicons? Do Bengalese finches sing a syntactically complex song? Yes; yes; beautifully, yes.

I look to a future when as writers we ask different questions and as readers we delight in the answers: How do other beings singularly and uniquely think, feel, experience, and speak? What shape does thought take when, for instance, it comes through many limbs, many suckers on many limbs, tasting and touching? (How dimensional and textured, an octopus thought!) And go from there.

For now, *After Coetzee: An Anthology of Animal Fictions* begins with innovations and delights right where we are.

Here.

NOTES

1. J.M. Coetzee, *Elizabeth Costello* (New York: Penguin Books, 2003), 218.
2. Sight has been a guiding trope for the contemplative and reasoned throughout Western philosophy. We regard ourselves as *the* seeing and therefore reasoning animals. Tellingly, scientists use a sight-based experiment—the mirror test—to determine whether species of nonhuman animals may be considered self-aware (that is, in accordance with current human standards of self-awareness). Nonhuman animals who respond to reflections of markings on their bodies "pass" the test.
3. My dog deuteragonist was named Chester, and he liked to investigate snails in a bit of boulevard.
4. Susan McHugh writes that when, as a student, she interpreted a Wordsworth poem as expressing a squirrel's perspective, her professor responded with exasperation. "Animals don't think, and they certainly don't write poetry," he replied. Susan McHugh, *Animal Stories: Narrating Across Species Lines* (Minneapolis: University of Minnesota Press, 2011), 5.
5. Radical black thinkers have long exposed the conceptions of animality that subtend, and are deployed by, operations of conquest against humans. For a brief overview, see Che Gossett, "Blackness, Animality, and the Unsovereign," Verso Books Blog, accessed November 20, 2016, http://www.versobooks.com/blogs/2228-che-gossett-blackness-animality-and-the-unsovereign. Ecofeminism in the mid-to-late twentieth century theorized the connections between the degradation of women, the environment, and nonhuman animals, culminating in Carol J. Adams crucially accenting consumption of "food animals." Carol Adams, *The Sexual Politics of Meat: A Feminist-Vegetarian Critical Theory* (New York: Continuum, 2010). Today, feminist philosophers working within the care tradition are expanding that framework to articulate ethics for nonhuman animals. See Lori Gruen, *Entangled Empathy: An Alternative Ethic for Our Relationships with Animals* (New York: Lantern Books, 2015). Powerful critiques are also emerging at the intersection of critical disability studies and critical animal studies. See Sunaura Taylor, *Beasts of Burden: Animal and Disability Liberation* (New York: The New Press, 2017), published as of this book's printing.
6. Posthumanism in this sense is, as Cary Wolfe writes, a "decentering of the human" and a reconsideration of the ways humanist "values and aspirations are undercut by the philosophical and ethical frameworks used to conceptualize them," particularly with regard to nonhuman animals. Cary Wolfe, *What is Posthumanism?* (Minneapolis: University of Minnesota Press, 2009), xv, xvi. For an overview of the philosophies that inform a Wolfian posthumanism, and an incisive analysis of the

challenges and opportunities those philosophies afford animal ethics, see Matthew Calarco, *Zoographies: The Question of the Animal from Heidegger to Derrida* (New York: Columbia University Press, 2008).
7. Brill Book's critical animal studies series, edited by Helena Pedersen and Vasile Stănescu, succinctly defines the field: "By 'critical' we mean that animal studies must not become a safe and sanitized discourse; it must...advance a radical and oppositional dissent that engages and politicizes the many profound ethical, environmental, and social issues embedded in animal studies." See "Critical Animal Studies," http://www.brill.com/products/series/critical-animal-studies. For a recent overview of critical animal studies, see Nik Taylor and Richard Twine, *The Rise of Critical Animal Studies: From the Margins to the Centre* (New York: Routledge, Taylor & Francis Group, 2014).
8. Of course, I am referring to literary writing and its attendant concerns, from genre to figuration. Posthumanists may discuss works of literature in theorizing the question of the animal, but their modes and approaches will necessarily differ from that of a novelist and literary critic. With Jürgen Habermas, I honor the distinctness of literature.
9. J.M. Coetzee, *Disgrace* (New York: Penguin Books, 2008), 25.
10. Ibid., 215.
11. Pat Harrigan, "Accepting What's on Offer in *Disgrace*," in William E. McDonald, ed., *Encountering Disgrace: Reading and Teaching Coetzee's Novel* (Columbia, S.C: Camden House, 2010), 110.
12. J.M. Coetzee, *Disgrace*, 215.
13. Ibid., 142.
14. Ibid., 146.
15. The novel's formal elements suggest so: the chapters number twenty-four, the same number as that of the dogs Lurie helps euthanize. The bodies of the figurative dogs help frame the body of the made book.
16. Matthew Calarco, "Toward an Agnostic Animal Ethics," in Paola Cavalieri and Peter Singer, eds., *The Death of the Animal: A Dialogue* (New York: Columbia University Press, 2009). Typical approaches to "animal ethics" would have moral considerability extended *from* humans *to* those beings who share qualities that are deemed human. As Kelly Oliver writes, basing "our ethical obligations to animals ...on their similarities to us reinforces the type of humanism that leads to treating animals—and other people—as subordinates." Kelly Oliver, "Animal Ethics: Toward an Ethics of Responsiveness" *Research in Phenomenology* 4 (2010): 267.
17. Matthew Calarco, "Toward an Agnostic Animal Ethics," 78. In his depiction of the encounter, Calarco adapts Emmanuel Levinas's face-to-face relation. Levinas limits that relation to the human, against what his own thought would suggest. Calarco's agnosticism opens up that face-to-face relation to encompass the more-than-human.
18. In fact, Coetzee employed the Costello novels as a kind of encounter. For the Tanner Lectures on Human Values at Princeton University in 1997, he read the chapters that would compose *The Lives of Animals* rather than lecture in his own

voice. In so doing, he brought forward the appeal of social and political others: Elizabeth Costello; Kafka's ape-cum-scholar, Red Peter; and the real chimpanzee Costello thinks Red Peter is modeled on, Sultan.
19. J.M. Coetzee, *Elizabeth Costello*, 96.
20. J.M. Coetzee, *Elizabeth Costello*, 98.
21. J.M. Coetzee, "Notes on Issues Raised by Matthew Calarco," in Paola Cavalieri and Peter Singer, eds., *The Death of the Animal: A Dialogue* (New York: Columbia University Press, 2009), 89.
22. J.M. Coetzee, *Elizabeth Costello*, 98.
23. Costello's self-scrutiny parallels, underscores, and doubles Coetzee's own doubling back, what David Atwell calls "doubling the point" in the collection of essays and interviews by that name. J.M. Coetzee, ed. David Atwell, *Doubling the Point: Essays and Interviews* (Cambridge, Mass.: Harvard University Press, 1992), 3. This doubling sometimes effects an underscoring of a theme or idea and sometimes a reconsideration of a work's premises and promises, performing a metafictional ethics of recursive self-scrutiny, of auto-debugging. For instance, in reading those chapters for audiences, Coetzee would have voiced not only Costello and her fellow primates, but her detractors. J.M. Coetzee—John—would have voiced Costello's son—John—thinking about his mother: "A strange ending to a strange talk, he thinks, ill gauged, ill argued." J.M. Coetzee, *Elizabeth Costello*, 80.

    Costello's *suspicion of self-certainty* does not become the *uncertainty of skepticism*, however, perhaps because Costello is always guided by "fidelities." J.M. Coetzee, *Elizabeth Costello*, 224. I take fidelity to be an agonic line, priming and directing the "sympathetic imagination" toward the object of its truest concern (ibid., 80). With Costello, Coetzee perhaps solves the problem he identifies in Samuel Beckett's work: the problem of uncertainty becoming a "phrase-by-phrase" dissolution of meaning and even of consciousness. J.M. Coetzee, ed. David Atwell, *Doubling the Point: Essays and Interviews* (Cambridge, Mass.: Harvard University Press, 1992), 44.
24. J.M. Coetzee, *Elizabeth Costello*, 90. For instance, she offers two poems by Ted Hughes as exemplar, but confesses that his ecologicalism taints the poems' otherwise energetic "bodying forth" of the jaguar and their engagement with "the creature itself." Too, "despite the vividness and earthiness of the poetry, there remains something Platonic about it." J.M. Coetzee, *Elizabeth Costello*, 97-99. Costello also admits that Hughes's poetry is the sort hunters would like—hardly an endorsement, coming from a vegetarian.
25. For Jacques Derrida, the category of "The Animal" has no ontological essence; it functions as a diversion from the unanswerable question of what *humans* are: "From within the pit of that lack, an eminent lack ... man installs or claims in a single stroke ... his superiority over what is called animal life." Jacques Derrida, *The Animal That Therefore I Am*, trans. David Wills (New York: Fordham University Press, 2008), 20. Thus, "it follows that one will never have the right to take animals to be the species of a kind that would be named The Animal, or animal in general" (ibid., 31).

26. His name notwithstanding, Mr. Crow has the markers of a human character, while the cat is thingified by the pronoun "it."
27. In fact, I had established several ethical parameters, winnowing out pieces that casually referenced human consumption of animal-based food or treated oppression as a neutral social fact. In the end, I did accept a few contributions that would appear to violate those parameters, but they largely use such moments to indicate an atmosphere of ignorance, if not malevolence, and the ways hierarchies self-replicate and oppressions interlock.
28. J.M. Coetzee, *Elizabeth Costello*, 79.
29. Derrida, *The Animal That Therefore I Am*, 18.
30. The forms of communication we take to be "human" *or* "animal" are rather more shared. Though some approaches to the study of language now "[put] forward a minimal account of human uniqueness," approaches in general begin with the assumption that human language is the standard by which other communications should be measured. Robin Dunbar and Louise Barrett, *Oxford Handbook of Evolutionary Psychology* (Oxford: Oxford University Press, 2007), 673.
31. Wiseman's piece recalls the critical work of scholar Susan Fraiman, who is concerned to recuperate the feminist origins of animal studies. See Susan Fraiman, "Pussy Panic Versus Liking Animals: Tracking Gender in Animal Studies," *Critical Inquiry* 39, no. 1 (2012): 89-115.
32. Marc Bekoff, *Animal Passions and Beastly Virtues: Reflections on Redecorating Nature*. (Philadelphia: Temple University Press, 2006), 26.
33. J.M. Coetzee, *Elizabeth Costello*, 74. Of primatologist Jane Goodall's bodily attunement to chimpanzees, Susan Griffin writes, "She hunkers. She sits in a hunkering attitude. We learn the attitude of not hunting. The attitude of learning." Susan Griffin, *Woman and Nature: The Roaring Inside Her* (New York: Harper & Row, 1978), 198.
34. See Victor Shklovsky, "Art as Technique," in David H. Richter, ed., *The Critical Tradition: Classic Texts and Contemporary Trends*, 3rd ed. (Boston: Bedford Books, 1998), 774-784.
35. J.M. Coetzee, ed. David Atwell, *Doubling the Point: Essays and Interviews*, 368.
36. Michel de Montaigne, *The Complete Essays*, trans. Donald L. Frame (Stanford: Stanford University Press, 1958), 397.
37. Most often published as "Strider" in translation. See Leo Tolstoy, *Collected Shorter Fiction: Volume 1*, trans. Louis Maude, Aylmer Maude, and Nigel J. Cooper (New York: Knopf, 2001).
38. Mark Twain, *The Complete Short Works of Mark Twain*, ed. Charles Neider (New York: Doubleday, 1957).
39. In her introduction to *Women, Destruction, and the Avant-Garde: A Paradigm for Animal Liberation*, Kim Socha argues that, in fact, children's literature functions to prime children to accept human supremacism. Kim Socha, *Women, Destruction, and the Avant-Garde: A Paradigm for Animal Liberation* (New York: Rodopi, 2012), 31.
40. Contemporary literature's disavowal of the more-than-human was not entirely complete, thanks in large part to feminists. For instance, in Alice Fulton's poem

"Some Cool," a farmer describes the routine abuse of pigs: "about electric prods and hooks / pushed into every hole. / About: they cried so much he wore earplugs." Alice Fulton, *Sensual Math* (New York: W. W. Norton & Company, 1996), 13. See also Patricia Highsmith's anthology of animal-revenge fiction, *The Animal-Lover's Book of Beastly Murder* (London: Virago, 2014) and Deborah Levy's polyphonic *Diary of a Steak* (London: Book Works, 1997), which imbricates constructions of "female hysteria" with consumption of animal bodies by voicing the madness of a BSE-infected steak.
41. Aldo Leopold, *Round River: From the Journals of Aldo Leopold*. (New York: Oxford University Press, 1953), 164.
42. In *Dog*, Susan McHugh asserts: "The problem"—the actual problem—"facing everyone who writes about dogs is that there are thousands, if not millions, of people who have already done so." Susan McHugh, *Dog* (London: Reaktion Books, 2004), 7.
43. We may speak of the diaspora of "wild animals" escaping polluted oceans and lands, but what of "farmed animals"? In the first place, what is their homeland?

AFTER COETZEE

NUMBER 2 PENCILS FOR THE WHITE CAT

Kyoko Yoshida

Mr. Crow is a corporate accountant, but, to tell the truth, he is a closet novelist. Whenever Mr. Crow runs out of ideas to write about, he switches his polished ebony fountain pen to a number 2 school pencil to return to the basics, to feel the friction that every word creates on the paper.

Mr. Crow lines up new number 2 school pencils on his writing desk, and, ritualistically, he sharpens each pencil with his pocketknife, at his desk by the window.

Wooden shavings fall into the dustbin he holds between his knees. He concentrates on the sound that the knife and the wood make. He inhales the friction heat and the mixed odor of ebony and clay that rises from the tip of the pencil.

Every time Mr. Crow sharpens his number 2 school pencils, every time he has writer's block, a white cat comes to the window, attracted by the calm, regular rhythm of the pencil sharpening. Then the cat sits by the window and stares at Mr. Crow's hands steadily sharpening the number 2 school pencils. The white cat is mesmerized by the movements of Mr. Crow's hands, the way the pencil is tilted, how the wooden shavings shed off the pencil like autumn leaves.

One night, when Mr. Crow is sharpening his pencils, not knowing what to write as usual, the white cat comes to his window as usual. This time, the cat is so mesmerized that it meows in an ecstatic yet scary voice, turning upside down, lying on its back. Mr. Crow opens the window for the first time. The white cat presses its cheek hard against the pencil in Mr. Crow's hand, sniffs the ebony and clay, licks its tip, and starts to bite and eat the pencil.

Half an hour later, the white cat finishes all the number 2 school pencils on Mr. Crow's desk. It looks up at Mr. Crow, burps three times, and starts to tell him the following story:

Here I omit the story for editorial purposes.

The dawn comes and the cat finishes its story. Of course, Mr. Crow writes the story down frantically. He publishes it. The story becomes a national bestseller. It is translated into thirty-six languages. Since Mr. Crow doesn't have writer's block anymore, he doesn't sharpen pencils. He writes with his new Mont Blanc. He has a dozen Mont Blancs. Since he doesn't sharpen number 2 pencils anymore, the white cat doesn't visit his study window.

Five years go by.

Now Mr. Crow has published ten more novels. He has moved into a mansion in Connecticut. He lives there all by himself.
One full-moon night in October, the white cat visits Mr. Crow's studio window, though Mr. Crow is not sharpening

pencils. The cat stares hard at Mr. Crow through the window pane.

Mr. Crow senses right away that the white cat wants to be repaid for Mr. Crow's success. He is afraid the cat will demand his first-born child. But he doesn't have any children since he doesn't have any wives or mistresses. So Mr. Crow tells the white cat in the gentlest way possible that he cannot offer the cat his first-born child. The cat stares at him without a word and walks away.

Afterward, the white cat starts to come uninvited to Mr. Crow's window.

"What do you want?" Mr. Crow asks, "My soul? My money? Tell me!"

But the cat says nothing. Its face shows no expression. It stares at him and goes away.

Two years later, Mr. Crow finds the white cat dead under the fallen maple leaves in his back yard. It is then that he realizes the white cat wanted more pencils.

More number 2 pencils for the white cat.

But it is too late.

OUR FATHERS, WHICH AREN'T IN HEAVEN

W.P. Osborn

The zealots wanted him for an icon, the national football team for a mascot, and Gyan Gana Gar, whose farms he had beset and whose headman had brought him to the attention of the larger authorities, a share of his future revenues in compensation. His constituencies, in short, made it difficult to budge him. Yet we thought him to exist under perils they hadn't recognized—of beggars eating him, of smugglers grinding him into philters to be dispensed in the markets of Phnom Penh or Marrakech. And we? We had veterinarians; we had guards to prevent depravity. In the end, we convinced at least the more legitimate factions that in Gyan Gana Gar he was a wasted quantity, while here in our Kapital Zoo he would be cherished. Of course, we also felt that if we accomplished it properly, he would improve our rate of attendance.

To what proper accomplishment amounted was a question we focused on through the seasons of the cold and the wet. To begin with, where would we show him? Some thought we should displace the hippopotamus. Others reminded us that the hippopotamus had been the entrance attraction perpetually—that moving him would squander the treasure we'd spent in publicity and advertisement. The public was best brought into the familiar before it dispersed to observe the strange, they argued. Besides, even if we relocated the hippopotamus, our new acquisition might turn out to be too large for the enclosure.

In addition to eighteen varieties of hummers and the requisite cloister of penguins, we owned flufftails, gallinules, jacanas, boubous, olyflysters, shrikes, and bustards. Unfortunately, the birds had never attracted attention enough to earn their board, and so, though it would have to become remote enough that our visitors could not be expected to put in the long effort it would take to get there, we thought of shifting the aviary. A fresh locale implied new transport, and the prospect of a photogenic, non-polluting monorail diverted us until it became apparent that in the most liberal calculations its construction could not be amortized over the new revenues expected from he who had fostered our discussion. Our options finally came to but one. We must modify the pachyderm compound, which was over beyond the rhinoceros, down near the cats. To be sure, it was a little out of the way, but we convinced ourselves that what visitors exerted themselves briefly to get to, they would appreciate all the more. We wanted to present him in the foreground there—to use the current pachyderms for his foil, as it were. We considered advertising him alongside our hippo. Eventually we could phase the hippo out. It might really be prudent to, as he was lately showing a disappointingly negative life attitude—not pitching in as we had come to count on him to do.

To open space for the construction, we drove the two varieties together. For a few days these segregated themselves and fed and watered at different moments, and it all went so well that we wondered why we hadn't combined them before. But then came a spate of overnight tuskings and there was nothing for it but to dart the worst-off until they rolled over and their trunks stretched out along the ground.

The carcasses were such a long reach for the crane that, though the operator installed extra ballast and hyperextended his outrigger, the weight began to tip it. We tried dragging them with block and tackle, but nothing would serve as a proper anchor. In finding this out, we bent signposts, smashed a vending machine, and dislodged a fire hydrant, the resultant flood inundating our dromedary down in Kraal 15. When we finally began to saw them up, a *Loxodonta* bellowed and flung the chief keeper and the night watchman against the fence. The former she knelt on. The latter we might as well have left to her as well, because in the presence of any big animal from that day forth, his joints were aspic. We did try him in the herpetarium, but he couldn't see the pythons without fainting.

The chief of the pet food factory didn't know whether dogs would want the meat, nor did she wish to edit the labels if she was going to have to change them back again when the supply ran out. She couldn't guarantee the approval of the Dietary Safety Panel. She hadn't the machinery to render a product so very large.

At the state landfill we were directed to the hazardous waste area. Who could say, the official reasoning went, how the gulls might be influenced by the consumption of this unfamiliar food, or where they might drop their contaminated guano? Who knew which rodent or insect might carry something untoward into the food chain? We were assessed to have our dead entombed in concrete, therefore, and it may accurately be said that by the time we buried them, we had had quite enough. All this trouble, and the flies accumulating by the minute, and a dank stink for our dreams, and we had yet to arrange the replacements for our three fallen comrades-in-arms.

For so we thought of them—they and we, bulwarks against a sometimes fickle public, warriors, each with a duty within an army, navy, or air force under the command of a General Zoo Administration interacting with the government to assure the maintenance of this place in the way best to attract the foreigners who could help sustain our nation-state. And why did this responsibility fall upon the zoo? Well, our heavy manufacturing was disappearing, the factories still warm taking continual losses in the certainty that the economic pendulum must eventually swing us back into the old prosperity. Of course, now that the wars were over and our enemies become our friends—now that our friends supplied us with better than we had ever produced, and at a cost our workers were unable to match . . . well let us respectfully remind our chief operating officers, our petit bureaucrats, plutocrats, and commissars, that the pendulum to which they referred was but a metaphor, and a metaphor is not obliged to imitate what it is supposed to represent.

2.
The rain jabbed down in needles, the macadam near the harbor reflecting the dim overhead lights in geometries of pale blue and ochre. The air before dawn smelled of grease,

of rusted iron, sweated wool, fried eggs, and petrol. Set off from the rest of the unloaded cargo of the ship to which we were directed was a crate. The slats were closely spaced, and we couldn't see any more than here a wrinkle, there something vaguely curving. Nearby it was warmer, and we knew from the odor that some of the waste was fresh. We could hear the draw and release of breath, the unmistakable huff which is the evidence of this animal's patience and curiosity. Our hearts accelerated.

Yet in the backs of our minds stood the common donkey, painted a zebra, the zebra retired and set to work as an ass, the ass then turned as sport to a Jungfrau. Or take the silent manatee, pawned off as a woman-fish to draw men to the sea. Put another way, we were mindful of the potential for mercenary transformation and we would not squander our resources on subterfuge. However, our agents overseas had written of the tests they'd performed to verify the special claims which had been made about him. They told us that only when they were sure he was what he'd been purported to be had they encouraged him out of Gyan Gana Gar, into the surrounding pineapple fields, six days up through the nut and mango groves, and onward off to the coast. There in Byoy Roshi, our agents and the mahout rotated a constant watch until the moorings were drawn and the craft, called *Pdylip*, drifted off the dock. At the destination, late, the papers indicating propriety, and those of us there to receive him suffering by then the irritability of expediency, we signed our names and impressed our seals and took possession.

So now, on the pavement of Zoo Trail Seven, under the lucent overcast of a late afternoon in the early leaf-fall, the crate containing our long-sought arrival finally stood. The rain had quit, but the air was thick with moisture, and the spikes, as one of the keepers prised them out, groaned and squealed like live things. When the upper forepanel came off, the new beast's eye was revealed, and we felt taken in by it. For though, granted, he looked nominally lighter than the usual shade, still he was of much the same dusky gray as his new sisters. In the distance a peacock howled. Nearer by, the monkeys laughed and we heard the bawling of a wildebeest and the assenting grunts of the stoat. We wondered what our representatives had been thinking. Had Gyan Gana Gar's resistance to our inquiries come out of a moral reluctance to part with him, as we'd been led to believe, or had it been a ploy to raise the price of an animal not far beyond the ordinary? When the back panels came away, there he was, and all our conference and expense, and the deaths of three decent specimens and one useful man, and the reduction of another into an imbecile, we now saw as the reflection of our false self-importance. The animal snuffled the mahout's coveralls and then followed him unprompted with his long, pacific stride down to the rear of his new-made enclosure, through the steel gateway, and straight along inside.

3.

Here were the teachers with their clipboards, counting and recounting the milling local children and rounding up their cowlicked strays. Most of the adults—mechanics, exotic dancers, disutilized assemblers and who-not—sat in arcs of folding metal chairs. On the temporary platform before them was a dais with a multitude of microphones. The governor would speak of the soon-expected economic improvements to which the zoo would be a prime contributor. Then the mayor, to congratulate us on this fresh jewel in a crown already encrusted with animal and scientific fame. Then Gyan Gana Gar's headman, to relate three tales of a beast who had once resided in a foreign clime where he had been considered to embody the holy. Then the head of GEZA, to describe with much humor the difficulties in obtaining him, and to thank the representatives of Gyan Gana Gar, and to congratulate us on our accomplishment; the president of the booster club, to inform all of the role of a zoo in conserving the species, and of the importance of overall zoo awareness, and to remind us of the availability of really very reasonable special memberships; and a generic advisor of the spirit, to eulogize man and beast lost in service to the cause and to bless our latest acquisition.

It was a warm middle of the day, the new leaves suspiring under not a breath of breeze. We heard the tootling of the calliope and the chug and whistle of the miniature train. The speakers spoke, the photographers shot, and the newscasters tested their angles and equipment and smoked, and all was a long awaiting, the carefully constructed anticipation beginning to wilt, hats removed and replaced, brows wiped with the backs of arms already slick with sweat, a baby wailing, the scents of corn sausage and popcorn, a woman off to the side in watch cap, pea coat, and laceless boots displaying a cardboard sign painted *Stop Animal Cruelty!* led away by security, late arrivals peering for empty seats and settling for the periphery under the fig trees, and at last, at last, at last, at last the moment when our crane, off to the side and good for at least this simpler task, starts its engine and, exhaling a puff of acrid smoke which immediately settles over the crowd but ends up, as it disperses, adding to the illusion of revelation, lifts the blue canvas arras, leaving only the wooden frame, the proscenium for our improvised stage. And standing under it, unaffectedly munching a mawful of fresh timothy, and then stepping forward onto the middle of the apron as if cued to do so, is the animal we have not yet permitted to be depicted in our publicity.

A moment of skeptical observation. It is not so big. It is wrinkled, but this is as one would expect. Its tusks may be undamaged, yes, but they're a bit—what do you think?—on the narrow side, right? for a male?

Then the conversation shifts. The eyes—these are not the brown we'd have expected here, but a shiny dark red. And look! What skin! Now that is something truly!

Programs which we've taken the trouble to have printed in four colors as souvenirs are dropped to the pavement. Viewers cover their hearts with their hands. They lift binoculars as the animal sits back and raises his forelegs and swirls his trunk. If a rumble were not heard from the darkening western sky, those in attendance might wish to overstay. As it is, they pack up, but pausing to gaze back into the new enclosure. For excepting the patch of rose at the shoulder and another across his forehead—the results of our perhaps overzealous scrubbing away at the grime of his transshipment—he is all over of the purest, the shiniest, the most pristine and milkish white.

4.

In order to remain the planet's finest zoo, we replicated conditions for natural living. All these beasts foraged on the imported *Arundo donax* we planted everywhere it would root. They lived in the shade of banyan, mangrove, and tamarind, which they trimmed or devoured as they pleased. They had at their disposal pools of clear water refreshed by artificial waterfalls. Our new acquisition wandered the capacious semicircularity of his new home, from the boulders at the rear to the trench at the front, pawing the outcrops of rock and vegetation, drinking, eating, snuffling the ground. At certain smells he retracted his mouth, lending his face the convivial expression so often seen in celebrity magazines. Visitors could at the same time they were watching him watch also the grays, giving them the illusion of depth, of abundance, almost as if they were out in the veldt. He too observed the grays. He stood looking at them, sometimes raising his trunk or bobbing his head. The adults didn't heed him. Our one calf, however, came near and bawled until he was jostled back into the group. A habitual interaction developed, the white chucking the little gray, mock jousting with him, assuming an attitude we saw as avuncular. And except for one potential problem, we speculated that if the barrier between them were removed, they would be all the better off.

Reports would occasionally reach us of a beast bringing down a circus tent and lumbering onto metropolitan avenues, citizens scattering before it, the authorities in disarray behind. It would have crushed automobiles, or butted down a light standard, or crashed through a storefront. Such wildness came, of course, from musth—a phenomenon exclusive to males. Our calf would experience this someday, and our new bull certainly already had, and would again. We could not really think of allowing the two to live together. We could not risk their harm. It did occur to us that if the adult could be brought into congress with the females, we might be able to put away the rubber-plastic-and-steel equipment that after a hundred experiments had brought us only the one little one. Perhaps we would end up with an expressed recessive gene.

The taciturn mahout chose this moment to interject an account of a Florentine beggar in possession of certain goblets. They were purple. They had been part of a larger number, perhaps several dozen in all, blown, etched, and gilded to the specifications of one of the Medicis by an artisan who disappeared soon after. Only the three in the beggar's possession remained extant, and the beggar knew their worth must be significant. He was actually on his way to the pawnbroker to inquire, when he experienced a sudden illumination, a feeling we might refer to in these latter days as the capitalist instinct. What would happen to the value, he wondered, if he hadn't his three goblets, but only one? Though perhaps a spectacle, to duplicate our acquisition through live birth, our teller meant to suggest, would be to create the penultimate goblet. He led us to a change of mind.

During this time, representatives of the stratum of society that collects erupting volcanoes, live hurricanes, and double eclipses toured our facility. We remember because we met with them and were photographed. Of course, they weren't the only ones who came, as word of mouth and the reports in the media built us into a sensation.

OUR FATHERS, WHICH AREN'T IN HEAVEN | 17

We posted on our kiosks the mail he generated, some of it quite touching. A boy, living on his family's farm to the south of Baden, inquiring whether the animal wouldn't like to visit. A widower in Du Lang, telling of a daughter's crooked spine which might be straightened if she could tickle the creature's belly. It was thought well to publish some of the letters in a booklet we could feature in the souvenir shop, the proceeds to defray the wages of the calligraphers we hired to answer them.

Schools relocated their curricula. The children assembled before an exhibit, at the picnic arbor, or in the viny courtyards, taking an unparalleled interest in the problems presented in their lessons. If a creature has a prehensile tail, what is its continent of origin? How is a water baby like and unlike a trout? In which ways might the tsetse be superior to the rhinoceros? Why does the tiger not prefer vegetables, especially popcorn? What are four wombats times thirty-seven howler monkeys? Please translate *Hakuna ruhusa ya kupita hapa mkubwa wa hifachi peke yake.*

A local radio station initiated a competition to name him. Other media imitated, and we began to receive the contenders. As it turned out, selecting the appellation by which he would become known was not a simple task. We tried. We arranged the entries in categories referring to size, color, individual part, emotion caused in the nominator, and qualities of leadership. Taken together, the groupings pointed out what a multifarious being we'd acquired. To choose one category, and from this a single name, was to eliminate all other categories and all other names, and thus to reduce, if not him—for in spite of everything, he was always to remain himself—then the way a visitor perceived him. Besides, we thought each name about as fine as the next. We spoke of selection by lot, but we decided that that would betray the good faith of the contestants. After a day and night of talk and stimulants, it came down to two choices. One faction thought we should refuse to select—for we hadn't sponsored the competitions and were only convened out of good sportsmanship. If he went nameless, they argued, he would remain appropriately undelimited.

The second faction advocated all the names together.

Ridiculous, the first group responded. How can you name something everything?

The list is not infinite, the second group quarreled. And recall the tradition elsewhere to provide newborn children with twenty-six names by the alphabet. Your question, which we take to be disingenuous in the service of scorn, may therefore reveal an accidental, and we might say rather unseemly, parochial bias.

After two more days of talk, cups and smeared plates scattered along the table and stacked in the corners, the participants black at the eyes and chapped at the lips, scratching at armpits and new beards, sprawling on the floor, the tables, two or three, mouths agape, drooling, the conference room smelling in better moments like rancid milk, we reached a compromise. We would not name him, but would instead commission a plaque to provide, without comment, all the supplied finalists.

These events occurred, not all at once, but over a period long enough for his image to spread to the remotest parts;

a period long enough that those who would see, saw; a period during which he became quite our largest animal. We could well account for his expansion by the bushels of raw rolled oats, racks of bread, sheaves of bamboo shoots, bags of imported cleaned soil, and tanks of filtered water we fed to him ourselves, the delicacies he took from the plantings, and the film cartons, paper bags, beverage containers, and other items given him by visitors. On first seeing him, they not infrequently tossed their hats. He went after these with a gusto for which no one was ever able to account, shredding and devouring them as if they were both upsetting and delicious. Was he overweight? Not if he was as long as a fire truck. Not if, standing on his hind legs, he was able to look out over our expanded, remodeled food court to see the other creatures and beyond.

He was never what we would term shy, either, seeming after a period of adjustment to take pleasure in his public contact. As he acclimated, so too did our visitors. This was fortunate, because from human resources such as gate attendants and food servers, to physical plant such as road sweepers and comfort rooms, his success had taken us to the point that we were forced to sell time-sensitive tickets. Eventually, as the public became no longer quite astonished, the furor to be with him diminished, and they began to visit him less as the exotic they must show their comrades today, tomorrow, and the next day, and more as a very dear old personal friend to be visited on holidays and anniversaries.

Not that when they visited he didn't provide fresh entertainment. He acquired a pet, for example. On a certain Tuesday, there she simply was, a parti-colored housecat in a patch of sunlight between his forelegs, as relaxed and immobile as a muslin sack of kidney beans. She could sometimes be seen dipping her tongue in his pools as he stood waving his trunk to disturb the hovering mosquitoes, or licking her paws as she sat atop his massive shoulders.

5.
We found him one morning with his eyes ringed in mauve and glazed. He was ramming his sizable head into the boulders of his waterfalls. The visitors became concerned. Won't he hurt himself? He could use a tranquilizer. Well if they dart him, they should be careful about the dosage. He'll have to hold still, or they might miss the spot. What is the spot? Behind the neck. In the rump. Over the shoulder. None of the above—they'll give it to him orally. Oh sure they will—how are they going to get close enough to even try that?

He went to his pool and then came near the road and twisted his trunk. The spectators were happy to find him active. When they were all properly pressed against the guardrail—a girl turning to ask her mother a question, a fellow in a puggaree bringing a cinnamon naan to his mouth—the beast lowered the trunk and soaked them. He pulled apart a wheelbarrow and flung one of the handles, which caromed off a decorative boulder and upset a woman's soft drink, causing her to stumble backward over the bird displaying unnoticed behind her peahen-patterned blouse, spin through a family leaving the food counter with fresh sandwiches, and fall down and badly sprain her wrist.

On the fifth afternoon, a woman in a rose caftan heaved the rascal a bottle, and within a very few minutes he was loping his perimeter more cheerfully indeed. In the days following, he was therefore barraged with strong beverage of every kind. He resisted none of it, so in the afternoons till closing time, he would rumble and trumpet and march in place and shake himself and summersault and roll his scarlet eyes. The mornings naturally found him eying food and water he wasn't fit to take. He took to throwing earth up over his back and head, and what the visitors saw as a result was something impressively large, yes, they would have to admit to that much, but not at all the charismatic albino they had come to see.

What is going on down at your zoo there, then? the province proconsul soon wanted to know.

An unalterable natural phenomenon, we told him.

A phenomenon which doesn't permit you to deny the public what you've advertised they'll be able to encounter.

Meaning that though our revenues paid his salary, he, being an honest reflector of the popular will, would, if the problem went uncorrected, reduce our share of the distribution. We tried cleaning our miscreant remotely with the high-powered hose, but succeeded only in transforming a dusty animal into a muddy one. Then people accused us of the negligent management of a distraught beast. By the time he came out of his condition, vital damage had been done to our reputation. For though a minor new class of visitor arrived for the scandal, by families unwilling to pay to see a creature falsely promoted or to expose their children to animal maltreatment, and by the local schools immediately re-traditionalizing their curricula, we were shunned. We considered it fortunate that he hadn't broken through to the grays. If he had, we might have experienced renewed tusking. We built a second fence a bit beyond the first, and between the two we constructed a rock wall. Our giant other would stand on his hind legs to peer over, but at his size this was an undertaking. He was reduced, therefore, when the by-then-becoming-middle-sized little one called him, to holding out his trunk.

6.

In better times, the government would have siphoned from elsewhere to help us recover our equilibrium. But factories counting on an economic upturn and enterprises depending on the spending of the factory-employed were going defunct. Our snarling, stalling, overheated-drivers-gesturing streets had emptied, until the limousines of government officials, moving as if elegance and speed could stimulate a renaissance, were nearly the only traffic.

We took action. We closed the restaurants. We let go faithful workers. We halved our salaries. Garaged the buses. Shut down the waterfalls. Tented the calliope, the little train. It was strange, what the zoo looked like then. Our new chimpanzee enclave was an unfinished sculpture. Animals awaited visits from a public failing to arrive. An uncanny silence hung over us, punctuated by the occasional roar of the lion or the snorting of the crocodile. The scents of spun sugar and charring wurst gave way to the redolence of unremoved waste.

We had heavy machinery and equipment for converting vegetable oil into frozen desserts, and we were considering what else we must sell in order to maintain our reduced existence. For a moment our communal ethic prevented us from thinking of the animals—for we were contracted to them, telling them, implicitly, never mind your captivity; it's a tradeoff—you're safe here, and so are any offspring; we know you have complicated relationships with others of your kind, just as we do.

But against the new reality such a code could stand for only so long, and thus we brought under discussion the Watusi cattle, the zebras, the camels, and yes, unfortunately, our tigers. As for the white, his diet was compromised now with bedding hay. Maintaining him was expensive, and the offers we received for him became more tempting. The argument against accepting them came down to the question of what our zoo was—thus, finally, of who we were. We'd sold the many. We had to preserve the few in order to entice back the visitors when the time came. And if the time never came, someone asked, where would the good lie in our having kept them all then?

7.

As we had performed a walk-through the evening before, and as the zoo was still closed to the public, we knew the incident on Trail Seven had occurred the prior evening and that the culprit was an animal. Two of our specimen palms lay across the road. The side and front walls of the snack bar were crushed. Inside, rubble was strewn over the flooded slate floor and torn electrical cable dangled near the waterline. Dining room tables and chairs were scattered, windows broken, the creatures and the children of the mural besmeared. The rhinoceros came to mind, but we had observed him in his enclosure. Nor could it have been our lethargic old hippo. No, the likeliest candidate was of course a pachyderm. But one two three four five six seven eight, there they all stood, breathing fog, stamping against the cold, seeming as benign as we were, if not as perplexed.

The mahout brought to his nose some waste from the road, then looked sharply at the white. He peered at the ground in front of the enclosure and was under the railing, squatting near the edge of the ditch, at his feet an imprint so large, there could be no doubt of whose it was. Now he was inside, conveying his disappointment, the creature bobbing and waggling and seeming by sign or in his nearly subsonic rumbling to answer back in inquiry. He nuzzled him and pawed the ground, but finally, under a dressing down which wouldn't stop, he lowered his head and large yellowish tears began rolling down his face and falling and soaking into the ground.

The mahout, who had called an urgent meeting, asked us to observe that the plaster castings in the cases along the wall were immaculate, while the one displayed just now on the long wooden conference table was reddish at the base. We speculated that it had been exposed somehow, and we wondered whether it had been used to create the footprint in the grass. However, we also believed the crime could have been committed by none other than our white. This is a problem with all systems of justice, the pressure to name a perpetrator causing impediments to thorough investigation and clear thinking. Certainly the white had in the past made his modicum of trouble, but we wouldn't convict him for a malady. Since our conscience told us we must now unconvict him, we realized we might have been too hasty to market him—the necessity to which we had finally surrendered on the day of the incident.

In the zoo, it is a few steps here, another few there, the mahout said, and what the wild wears away, the domestic cannot much influence. He touched the base of the casting and said, Please observe the manicured toenails, here, here, here, and here. Now come with me.

Soon he had the creature's left forehoof up on a drum. The toenails were long, uneven, and gnarled, our reduced staffing having kept them from the rasp. Too, we realized that the animal could not have made one print without leaving others, and that the ball of solid evidence in the road might simply have been moved there. Well, if he hadn't caused the wreckage, who had? And why?

Our contraction went on undisturbed by the trumpeting to which we'd occasionally been treated when he dwelt below, the distinct call which reminded us of the success we'd experienced in obtaining him, and of the remuneration we'd for a time received as a result. We had the relocation of numerous creatures still to think about, and we left his care entirely to the mahout, who moved him for convenience and security into a nearer enclosure lately belonging to the meerkats. Meanwhile, the Kapital avenues, formerly streaming with traffic passing by parklands planted in jacaranda and bird of paradise, had been occupied by looters. The nearer they approached, the sharper the motivation to slip off our remainder. This was the atmosphere in which we undertook a last discussion concerning his fate. The new enclosure was up behind us in a thicket. When we walked up to see him, he was lying on the ground with his back to us, torpid, gloomy, and dejected, as his cat had declined to come with him. The mahout informed us that after he helped load him onto the freight car, he meant to travel home.

8.
Here he is again! one of us will say now, and we'll gather to view his image in the newspaper—sometimes marching behind a wagon transporting a juggling bear, sometimes stolid beside a man with a painted face, sometimes, yes, encaged. Over time, the bones of his shoulders appear. Over time, the skin covering his ribs and hips begins to sag. Gradually, we see the bulky legs go bandy, the jowls emaciate, and the masculine tail shrink to stringiness. In recent pictures, the prominent eyelashes appear to have fallen out. His face is marred by descending black lines below the eyes. He is clean enough, but this is as it would be, his skin being what people pay their bits of money to look at—even though they know, because it is reported in editorials, that weapons are used to control him, and can see with their own eyes that his ankles are banded and hasped. We believe his trainer, with his prodding and withholding, is not aware of what the beast is capable. It may be he believes he has taught him the behaviors by which he entertains the public. The truth is that he performed many of them spontaneously. We once witnessed him conducting our grays in synchronized pirouettes, for instance.

He stands on a rubber ball without falling off; sops the shaggy men in their miniature cars; holds the ring of fire for the cougar to vault through; opens a peanut and hands the meat to the ringmaster. In the background of one picture we view the open mouths and waving arms of the children, the hovering parents and aunts seeming to say to their little charges, you will never encounter the like of him again. We can also make out on a few faces—not scowls, exactly, but the shades, we think, of doubt. To the towns he visits come epidemics of divorce and self-mutilation. Of course, the state scientists assure us that these are statistically insignificant anomalies.

It has proven impossible for our politicians to fix the position or even the direction of travel of our national fiscal pendulum. They can only tell us it is far from center and its return will take more time. Meanwhile, the stench of burning chemicals is ever stronger. When we begin to hear the crackle of small arms and the shouting of voices, we crank down the water main, switch off the power, close the cages, and cotter the turnstiles. No one doubts that our contentions, and even our crimes, have occurred under the determination to do right, and now that the work is ended and we are outside again, we are brothers. One of us recalls that late in the summer night, while Florence was sleeping, the mahout's beggar had gotten together the courage to hurl one of his goblets at the fountain in the marketplace. Someone else picks up the story: He tested the weight of the second and gritted his teeth, and then smashed it too, against a statue. A marble statue, someone chimes in—of the Duke of Padua. Yes, I remember, someone adds—he was on the cusp of enough wealth to carry him through the remainder of a life theretofore plagued with squalor. And just as he was pulling from his sack the last, most precious thing to show to the pawnbroker, a second customer rushed in; or perhaps he noticed across the pawnbroker's cheek the pale trace of an illegal dueling scar. As to the cause, the mahout was ambivalent, but the effect was the same. The only goblet slipped.

Big Thing, one of us muses after a long silence.

For we find ourselves standing outside with our hands in our pockets, facing the plaque of names we'd bespoken, patinaed now in verdigris, and likely to be torn away soon and thrown into the fires along with everything else of value in the Kapital.

Stands By Himself, reads another.

Torquemada, a third says.

We run through the nominations: Quasimodo. Monster Mash. Hannibal. Miràggio. Shogun. Taisho. Erector. Howdah. Flaps. Wish. Doughboy. The Mahatma. Honky Cat. Spuds. Buddha. Star of Gana Gar. Humpty. Fromage. Der Kaiser. A Light in the East. Caulk. Footprint. Long Lip. Saggy. Alieni Generis. Sueño de Miel. Bags. Curly. Acme. Apex. Onion. Knödel. Ekstase. Schnozz. Tusker. U1 Haole. Obruni. Rumble. Whitey. The Rebel. Dumpling. El Tio Blanco. Bright Angel. Kwai Lo.

And lift our shoulders and step off in separate directions.

THE GOAT

David Brooks

Whether the goat was as crazy as they'd been saying I just wouldn't know. Charging from out of nowhere, butting everyone from the property—there's always the chance it had good reason. The woman, too, seems to have been mad as a cut snake, but there could be reasons for that also. She had a different surname from her son, not that you can deduce much from that. And his hatred for women was all too clear. As for the goat, I can't imagine how it must have been feeling, suddenly abandoned, alone for all that time. One day the woman there, and the dog, the cat, and the next all gone. No explanation. Not that you can explain to a goat. Someone every few days bringing bread, every now and again someone else nosing around. I think I would have chased everyone off too, if only as a means of saying I'm here, I'm HERE. Though perhaps she'd trained it that way, the woman. Butting the son off the property every time he came. Animals can be more in sympathy with their human companions than most seem to imagine. Stockholm Syndrome. Hostages adopting the mind-set of their captors.

I didn't know anything about it, the goat, until ten days ago. Or rather had forgotten, almost completely, though had you asked me specifically if there was a goat in the neighbourhood I might have remembered Pauline telling me about it.

I had taken her some lemons, Pauline, since she'd asked for them, having seen the tree from the road, and she'd invited me in for a cup of tea. I was looking out her kitchen window, trying to think of something to say, and she talked about the way the roof of the house next door obscured the view. She's on the top of West Street, just as we are, on the other side, and the street, a cul-de-sac, slopes down so that the roof of the house next door is at eye level from Pauline's window. You can see into the tiny yard. It was then she told me about the goat. "I thought it was a compost heap," she said, laughing, "until I saw it move ... It's not there now. It spends most of its time under the house, when the woman's not there—she works during the day. At night I think it sleeps inside."

Pauline's the kind of person who takes notice of things, wants to know everybody. I think in the few months since she arrived she's got to meet more neighbours than we have in three years. But then we're different and keep to ourselves. Animal people. Pariahs. Not that we can see much of our neighbours anyway because of the thick ti-tree all down the West Street side. You can tell when there are cars there, and sometimes hear people, but nothing specific. For a while a taxi came, morning and night—it was never clear to which of the houses—and for a while more recently there's been the occasional ambulance.

I asked Pauline about her neighbour, while we were standing at the window, and was surprised to hear they'd never actually met. "I went down there a few days after I moved in," she told me. "The front door was covered with notices, and at the centre there was one in bold letters saying I'M AN EX-USER. I'M OFF MY MEDICATION, AND I'M ARMED, and another saying COME RIGHT IN! I'M ALREADY DISTURBED!" "When I read those," she said, "I figured she didn't want visitors."

The only other thing I knew—might have known, had I had any context for it—was from a piece of mail, about a month ago. A misdelivered letter, to a person whose name meant nothing to me, from a Cedar Lodge, on Riddle Road. When I realised it was for 4 West Street I thought I'd do the neighbourly thing and take it around. On my way it slipped from my hand and the contents shifted behind the window in the envelope, and I could read, above the name, "Acceptance of Resignation." Again, nothing that meant anything to me, though later I'd remember getting a taxi from the late train last year when the car was in for repairs, and the driver saying "West Street? No problem. I go there all the time," and telling me about a woman who worked in an old people's home on Riddle Road, who took a taxi to and from work every day.

There was a steep, sloping drive down through a mass of privet and cottoneaster to a rickety gate, a front yard full of weeds and long grass, and a dilapidated fibro cottage up on stilts. In the dark space below it I could see bike parts, an old bathtub, a discarded kitchen cabinet, but nothing you'd call a sign of life. A faded blue letterbox bearing the number 4 was wired to the telephone pole outside the gate. I slipped the letter in, imagining the addressee long gone. Maybe she'd won the lottery, or just got sick of the mountain cold. When a couple of weeks later we saw lights on in that house—something we had never realised we could see before, and mightn't have noticed even now if we hadn't been trying to work out the source of a loud car radio—we figured, ruefully, that it was new tenants, though as it happened the lights soon went out and the car drove off, and the house slipped back into its normal darkness.

And then, two weeks ago, I went to see Geoff down at the bottom of the hill, about his ewes getting out and coming up to tease our ram through the fence. He said there was a fresh hole in his own fence. He'd been meaning to fix it, just needed to get hold of some wire mesh. When I told him I had some—anything to speed him up—he said he'd come to collect it next time he was feeding the goat.

"The goat?" I asked, remembering now.

"Yes, the one at 4 West Street. The woman there has died and I've been looking after it."

"Died?"

"Yes. Cancer. She'd been in and out of hospital for a couple of months and I'd been looking after the goat for her—she got it from me in the first place—and she died two weeks ago."

It all suddenly added up. The resignation, the ambulance, the neglected house. I wondered where the goat had been when I'd taken the letter around. Certainly I'd seen no sign of it.

"There was a cat," Geoff continued, "and a little dog, but they've gone to other people already."

"And the goat's still there, by itself? Is someone trying to find it a home?" I can't always anticipate the questions Frieda will ask me but I could be pretty sure of this one.

"I've been asking around, but it butts, won't let anyone onto the property. There's a couple in Forestville might be interested. I called them but I haven't heard back."

I told Frieda when I got home and she was concerned straight away. "Poor goat!" she said, "It must be so lonely and confused!" I told her Geoff was trying to find it a home and she scoffed that he was too lazy to find his own fly buttons, said he was probably waiting a decent interval before eating it. She wanted to know how old it was, if it was a male or a female, what was its name, but of course those were questions I hadn't thought to ask. So immediately, brushing aside my warnings about the butting, she went around to see for herself. And of course went in, when she couldn't see it, and the goat was suddenly there, butting her. It is a large brown goat, she told me when she got back. I got no answer when I asked if she'd been hurt. She was too busy speculating about how we could find it a new place to live.

"And was it a male or a female?" I asked.

"I don't know. I didn't get a chance to see. It all happened so quickly. It had big horns. Isn't it the males that have the horns?"

"I don't know," I said. "I think both do."

The next morning she went to see Geoff, came back frustrated with how little he knew. The goat was a female but he had no idea as to her name, if she had one at all. The woman had always just called her "the goat." A purebred brown boar. She'd had her for seven years. And yes, the woman had children—or at least one—but he knew no name and had no contact details. He told Frieda that she could try giving the goat some bread, though he assured her she didn't need feeding. And that she should never turn her back on her.

"He couldn't even think of the woman's name! Can you believe it?" Frieda was incensed. "Though supposedly he's known her all this time! And I don't think he's got *any* plans for placing the goat at all." That evening, along with a few slices of sourdough—all the bread we had—she took the camera so that she could get a photo to put up on the internet, along with the call for a home.

"We also need a name," she said. "It'll be a lot easier if she has the right name." But then rejected everything I suggested. Too classical. Too literary.

She showed me the photographs. The goat had only appeared briefly from her place under the house, and she'd only managed to take two pictures before she went back there again. In one, taken from the side, the goat seems to be rolling her eyes and looks demented, but in the other she is front on, looking directly into the lens, and her sadness seems apparent, though who am I to say what a goat's sadness looks like? I live amongst animals and look into their eyes often enough, but not often as long as I looked into those.

That evening Frieda worked intently on the computer and around midnight brought me a carefully worded plea. The goat was now Molly, and the text spoke of her grief, her need for careful treatment and understanding. It spoke of her living alone under the derelict house, with no way of knowing what had happened to her human companion, deprived of the cat and dog that had been her only other company.

There was nothing about the butting. It seemed very effective to me. We agreed that the call should go out as it was and Frieda said she'd stay up to do it. As I was brushing my teeth she came in to the bathroom and began undressing to take a shower. There was a long, dark bruise on her thigh. When I remarked in concern she turned to show me an even longer one on her back. I know for a fact that she doesn't bruise easily. I went to sleep that night trying to remember what I could of *The Billy Goats Gruff,* and then thinking of the woman and her job at the nursing home, working all day amongst the seriously lonely, the seriously confused. What did she do when she came home at night to her cat, her dog, her goat? Did she read? Watch TV? Drink? And had she really been a user? This town is full of them.

When we got up there were already two or three responses to the internet notice, and others trickled in through the morning. Around noon Frieda called me from the study. I thought it was to see another offer, but it was to say that there were a couple of cars outside the woman's house—you can see a bit better from her study window—and that we should go down as it might be her children. Maybe we could find out more, or at least make sure we had permission to do what we were doing. We didn't want to rescue her and then find ourselves accused of stealing. As we descended the overgrown driveway two men, each somewhere in their mid-forties, emerged laughing from a back yard I hadn't noticed before. From the way one of them was gesturing about the place we guessed—correctly, as it happened—that this might be the woman's son, and introduced ourselves, explaining why we had come. He shook our hands, told us his name was Bernie, and said immediately that he was glad to see us and only too happy to have us find the goat a home. In truth, he said, we had just saved the goat's life. He'd found a home for the cat and the dog, but the goat was such a mean creature he figured no one would want it, and only that morning had decided to have it put down, but if we thought we could find someone crazy enough to take it we were most welcome. "I even asked my Middle Eastern friends who eat goat," he said, "but they didn't want a seven-year-old female." Its name was "Nut," short for "Nutley." He had always hated it, and had no idea why his mother was so attached to it. It was demented and potentially lethal. It would charge anyone who ever entered the yard except her. I asked his mother's name, now that he had mentioned her, and apologised that I did not know it already. "Sue-Ellen Jamison," he answered, offhandedly, as if it hardly mattered. If there was any grief hanging in the air it certainly wasn't coming from him.

At this point Frieda, who has what you could call a fine ear for character, had clearly heard enough and began to walk home on the pretext of checking something on the stove, leaving me to exchange contact details and ask what I could remember of the list of things we still needed to know. The man who had been with him—I figured he was a real estate agent—took this opportunity to make his own departure, and it seemed Bernie was about to leave also. We climbed the driveway and stood for a few moments by his car as he searched out a business card to give me. Over his shoulder I saw the goat come out from under the house—where had she been while Bernie and the other guy were there, and why hadn't she butted them?—and take a few tentative steps toward the gate. She was larger than I'd imagined, and walked in an odd, high-stepping way. When Bernie drove off—I was already halfway up the street by this—she gave a small bleat.

That was Thursday. All the next day we worked on the offers, trying to decide which would be best for a creature about whom the only thing we really knew was that she butted everyone who came near her. We settled at last on a place at the foot of the mountains, on the city side. There were already a couple of goats there, in a two-acre paddock. It seemed to us that that would give Molly the space she needed to sort herself out, without doing much damage to others. We called, spoke to the woman there, arranged to deliver Molly in our old van on Sunday. At some point in the early afternoon I heard a large truck going down West Street. There was a bit of clanging and banging. I thought nothing of it. Garbage trucks often have a bit of trouble negotiating the cul-de-sac. When Frieda came back from visiting Molly it was to report, along with the fact that she had eaten the bread and the lucerne she'd left for her the evening before, that a huge dump-bin had been delivered and placed right in the middle of the driveway. "How on earth," she asked, "are we going to load her into the van, with that thing there?"

It was going to be quite an operation. We'd have to pad the van somehow, to cushion an angry goat thrashing about in there—fill it with hay, use bales of it at the driver's end to protect ourselves from sudden attack from behind, and all this presuming we could get a belligerent Molly into the vehicle in the first place without getting ourselves a ruptured spleen or our hands torn to shreds by her horns. We called

Geoff. He said he'd be happy to help load her—though he didn't sound happy. He had a trick, he said, for calming her down. And music, he suggested, music in the van, or just the radio. She was probably used to the sound of the TV and might be calmed by the voices.

It had been a hot day and I went out after dinner to sit on the deck in the cool and the moonlight. I could hear the occasional bleat from one or another of the sheep in the bottom paddock, or from one of Geoff's flock a bit further down. Had Molly been bleating the whole time in her distress, and no one hearing her? I listened now, intently, to see if I could distinguished any sound from over there. Sometimes I thought I could but it was hard to tell one bleat from another, or a bleat of distress from any other kind. Perhaps they were all bleats of distress, from all over the valley.

The next morning we were woken by the steady thumping of things being thrown into the dump-bin, and by ten the house was full of the cloying smell of pesticide. They—whoever they were, and there were several by the sounds of it—were gutting the place, and fumigating as they worked. Fine, if they wanted to poison themselves along with the insects, but did they have to poison the neighbourhood along with them? I contemplated going over to protest but the thought of Molly stopped me. Best not to risk the re-housing by an argument with Bernie. Where was she in all this racket? Had they tied her up? At lunch, the smell still lingering about us, Frieda suggested I go to tell Bernie about the new home we'd found. One of those suggestions-without-option: there was no way she was going to do so.

I could see Bernie through the open sliding door. He

was standing at a table upstairs with several others, though the only one I could see clearly was a young woman, presumably his daughter. They were looking at something on the table—I imagined a photograph album, or a collection of records—and laughing and talking animatedly. Having a great time cleaning up grandma's. There was no immediate sign of Molly, though eventually I did see something shifting slightly in the under-house darkness. No doubt her sky-grey eyes had been staring at me the whole time, wondering whether I was just another intruder to be butted away.

Eventually Bernie saw me and came down, extending his hand as he approached. He was glad to hear of the new home, thanked us for finding it. He asked how we were going to take it there—he always referred to her as "it"—and apologised for the dump-bin, that was obviously going to create a problem in loading her. He explained that he wanted to get the house on the market as soon as possible, and had already had some evaluations. The real estate agents had said that house would best be displayed as empty as possible, given the general condition of the contents. Already—I was looking at it as he spoke—the bin was full of just about anything I could imagine being in a house: kitchen cupboards, an old double bed and exhausted mattress, a sofa, a TV, a pet's food bowl. He was very confident, he said, of selling the place for a good price. He'd thought it hardly worth putting on the market, but the first quotes he'd had had surprised him. It was a chance, he said, of recouping at last some of the money he'd lost in the settlement of his first marriage. And without my saying anything at all he was off. There was nothing so ferocious, he said, so *tenacious* as women. There was something *different* about them, something sinister, almost evil. And before I could think of a response had embarked upon a story of his daughter as a child. She had come to him sobbing because her younger brother had broken one of her toys. Nothing would console her, he said—and she *insisted* upon this—but his taking one of her brother's toys, his *favourite* toy, and breaking that. At this—there being something so compelling, so disturbing about this simple story—my mind was saying, "No, of course you didn't…"

But instead he said, "So I did. Nothing else would shut her up. I took his favourite toy and broke it in front of her, and as I did the weirdest, nastiest look came over her face…"

I got away, then, as quickly as I could—told Frieda about it when I got home and then tried to shut it from my mind. There was a lot to do, after all, to prepare the van. We did not have enough hay, to start with, and there was a search to be undertaken for cardboard boxes, to flatten and tape over the windows, to make sure Molly didn't hurt herself, and give her the darkness we felt, along with the music and a large supply of bread, might help to calm and distract her. There were also five or six metres of thick rope to be found, since—and I must admit the theory might have outweighed the practicalities—I'd worked out that, if we could get a fixed loop around Molly's head, one of us could hold one end, on one side of her, and the other the other end on the other side, so that we could counteract any attempt to butt or charge us as we unloaded her. We already had the old door we use as a ramp in loading the sheep.

In the end we needed almost nothing. Not the old door, not the music, not even the rope. At the designated time

Geoff was already waiting at the curb for us, with Molly on a dog leash. She seemed nervous, but also curious about what was happening. It was the first time I'd been so close to her. I saw straight away—it was as if we all noticed it at once—how misshapen her front hooves were. As if they had never been trimmed. No wonder she walked so strangely. After giving her a little time to settle and look into the van, Geoff and Frieda each took a front leg and lifted, while I pushed from behind, expecting all the time a kick in the face, but finding instead that she seemed to be trying to make my job as easy as possible. And the fifty-minute drive was much the same. At first she shuffled about, trying to keep her balance, but then lay down and we heard nothing more. No butting, no battering of the van. It was warm and we had the windows down. Driving through the Yarramundi Pass I heard the clear, crisp chink of bell birds.

The paddock she would now live in was one we could drive right into. A woman, her husband, and their teenage daughter met us, and after a brief conversation we all stood carefully back while Frieda opened the van door. After a few seconds just standing there, as if allowing her eyes to adjust to the light, Molly stepped calmly down, looked curiously about her—at the two white goats, the single sheep, the horse in the next paddock, the three large bull mastiffs observing curiously but quietly through an upper fence—and immediately began to graze. The woman noticed the hooves straight away and said firmly that they would have to do something about that. The daughter went off and came back with handfuls of lucerne. The man came over three times to rub Molly between the horns. I'd been envisioning a crisis but there had been nothing so far and no sign of one now. After a few minutes there seemed no reason to stay any longer. "You look after the gate," the woman said to her husband, as if to break a kind of spell, "while I take her up to meet the others."

She waited for us to close the back of the van, get in, and turn on the ignition, then, waving, turned her back and began to walk up the rise. Molly followed, docile and without bidding. Each of them high-stepping through the grass.

WHO IS THIS DIMAGGIO?

J.T. Townley

As if I have any other choice.

I'd like to topple a table lamp or slice a gas line to distract them long enough to escape, but the doors and windows are always locked. I've considered waiting for one or the other to leave, then slipping out behind him, only where would I go? Other ideas flit through my mind as I lie, half-starved, on the bare parquet. Poison, a blade across their throats in the night, a great conflagration. But I'm incapable of such acts, however hot my hatred may glow. (My heart is a blue flame.) Until now, I've bided my time, suffering their idiocy and counting the days.

But that's all about to change.

They take me for another Walk of Shame, their daily effort to quash my morale. My captor straps me into a harness, then parades me on a leash among screaming automobiles, shrieking babies, and callow canines, who laugh and bark and gnash their teeth.

"Think he really likes this, Farnsie?" That's the sidekick, Sheldon. His knuckles are hairy, his forehead simian. He never stops drinking from the aluminum cylinders they keep in a box filled with ice.

"I keep telling you, Shel," says Farnsworth, my captor. "He's a she."

"Then what's with the name?"

"What else should I call him?" My captor asks.

"Her, you mean."

We're through the door, and Farnsworth attempts to unbuckle the harness, but I refuse to let him near me. Not that I enjoy being stuck in it. But I have to take a stand, let them know I know what's going on, and, to the extent I'm capable, resist their scheming and machinations.

Then I realize: that's it. If not murderous vengeance, I have to show them what I'm capable of. My options are grossly limited; yet there must be some possibilities. So I focus on what they value. I think: aluminum cylinders. I think: glowing box. I think: incomprehensible game of balls and sticks and brightly colored uniforms.

And I know what needs to be done.

What I don't know is how, so nothing happens immediately. Even after the idea comes to me, slowly, as if from the bottom of a murky pond, it takes a while to communicate my intentions. I'm still groping toward them myself. Yet no matter how obvious my hints, neither notices anything. It's little wonder. They direct most of their energy at the glowing box, and the rest of it is given over to the chilled cylinders of Isopropyl, the stench of which reminds me of the torturer's office. Occasionally, they eat from cartons that smell of oregano and garlic, or ginger and soy sauce. (What they offer me is pasty dreck.) They're dullards, these two; it's frustrating.

But I can't go on counting the days of my captivity, so I breathe deeply and lower my expectations.

They stare at the glowing box for days on end. They notice nothing.

But then, one cool May afternoon, the sidekick emerges from his trance just long enough to say: "Look at her sitting there, Farnsie. DiMaggio's a regular Giants fan."

I used to think: Who is this DiMaggio? My name is Licorice; it's always been Licorice. It's what Lisa calls me, when it's not Sweetie or Sugar or Kitty.

Sheldon tilts his head back, pours chilled Isopropyl down his gullet. After crushing the aluminum cylinder, chucking it to the floor, and belching, he says, "You have any tuna?"

"Got the munchies?" my captor asks, tugging at a loose thread at the hem of his sweater vest. "We can order a pizza."

"No, Farnsie. I've got an idea."

After dumping out what's left in my bowls, he opens a can of tuna and places half in the orange one I use for food, the other half in the black water one.

Farnsworth pulls another aluminum cylinder from the box of ice. "So you're making tuna salad in DiMaggio's bowls?"

"No, wiseass," Sheldon says. I've got a feeling about this cat."

"A feeling?"

"What if she has powers, Farnsie?"

"Did you smoke something funny before you came over?" My captor asks.

The sidekick ignores him, placing my dishes on the floor near the glowing box. Then to me Sheldon says, "Don't listen to him. You're named after one of the greats. I believe in you."

I stroll over to investigate, sniffing at the canned tuna. I prefer fresh ahi, which Lisa gives me at least once a week. But this smells better than the usual muck.

Then Sheldon asks, "So who's going to win? The Giants?" He points to the orange bowl. "Or the Other Team?" He points to the black one.

I lean forward, sniffing at the black bowl.

"No hurry," says Sheldon.

"You've lost it," my captor says.

"Take your time," says Sheldon.

I nibble at the tuna in the orange bowl. It's past its prime, but that's not the point. Because, although I can't explain the details, I know where this is going.

"Giants!" Sheldon sounds excited. Then he asks: "Over or under?"

"You can't be serious," my captor says.

"Orange for over," he explains, "black for under."

I have no idea what he's talking about, but I understand that my opportunity has finally come. I feel drawn to the tuna in the black bowl, so I have a taste.

"Under!" shouts Sheldon. "Give me your phone."

"Don't do this," my captor says, handing him a black rectangular apparatus.

Sheldon disappears into the bedroom.

They're on tenterhooks after that. There's less laughter and more balled fists. Their sweat carries the rancid tang of fear.

I think: I've botched it.

I bury myself under my blanket in the corner and sink into a sour, disappointed sleep.

I'm startled awake by shouting. I'm groggy. The chorus of grunts and yells, all expressions of surprised elation, is deafening.

Sheldon leaves. Now my captor can't sit still. He paces the room, guzzling iced Isopropyl. He breaks into an arrhythmic jig in the middle of the room. He struts and flexes, admiring his reflection in the window. His antics are amusing. I imagine parading him through the park on a harness and leash.

Time passes; I give myself a bath.

At some point, Sheldon returns, staggering and singing. He's woozier than when he left. He passes a six-pack of aluminum cylinders to my captor, then tosses a greasy bag of fried food on the kitchen table.

"What took you so long?" says my captor. "Where's the money?"

The sidekick flashes a roll of green paper. It reeks of loneliness and desperation. It's a stench I know all too well.

My captor backhands drool from his lips. "The snacks come out of your cut," he says, then takes the roll and stuffs it into a grubby shoebox.

Tuna and predictions, hand-wringing and shouts of joy: soon it all becomes routine. And Sheldon always returns with green paper in stacks or wads or rolls. Insofar as I contribute to its accumulation, I become my captor's Most Important Concern, and rewards come with my newly exalted status. For instance, the Walk of Shame is no more; I haven't heard the clink of the harness buckles for what feels like ages. Gone, too, is the pasty glop, as well as the thin blanket on the bare parquet in the corner.

So I milk the situation for all it's worth. At night, I relegate Farnsworth to the sofa, luxuriating in the middle of the warm, soft bed. During my waking hours, I romp after the catnip mice they give me. And I eat with relish, especially on days when I perform my divinations, as my captor replaces canned tuna with fresh ahi. I even loll in the kitchen window, sunning myself and laughing at the dogs in the lawn below: they're chained to a post but think they have the world by the tail.

Also, the catnip; did I mention that?

One evening just before another incomprehensible game, my captor's black rectangular apparatus begins singing. He puts it to his ear; how doesn't that deafen him? Then I hear her: Lisa!

"There you are," she says. "Why're you avoiding me? I've been calling all day."

"Phone must've been off."

I follow my captor back to the bedroom.

"Okay, Farnsworth," Lisa says. "Where's my cat?"

"Our cat. When'd you get back?"

"You were supposed to have her here yesterday. Remember?"

"I know, sweetie," my captor says. "But—"

"Don't 'sweetie' me. We're not together anymore. Or did you forget?"

I follow my captor back to the kitchen.

"Listen, DiMaggio's started doing this amazing thing. We just need to keep her for"—he glances at Sheldon, who signals with two fingers—"a couple more weeks."

"Weeks?"

"Days! Days, honey. Just a couple more days."

My captor paces back and forth across the living room like a cornered mouse. I watch and wait.

"I am not your 'honey,' so don't call me that. And what do you mean 'DiMaggio'?"

"Licorice. I mean Licorice. It's just something we call her."

"Who?" Lisa demands. "You and your loser friend?"

My captor glances over at his sidekick, a grin tickling his lips. "He's not that big a loser."

"Does he even have a job? Do you?"

"I've taken a—leave of absence."

"From your senses, you mean?"

"Just until the season's over."

"When's that?"

"October."

"You're completely hopeless, Farnsworth. It's only May, for godsakes!"

Neither says anything for a moment. Static buzzes on the line. A muted catnip memory lingers on my tongue, mint green.

Then Lisa says: "Have Licorice here by five o'clock tomorrow, or I'm coming to get her myself."

"Don't get bent out of shape."

"And I'm bringing Bruce with me!"

The line goes dead. Bruce is a hulking giant who lives with Lisa and me. He enjoys lifting heavy objects.

Farnsworth rubs his face, takes a deep breath, then flumps down onto the sofa next to his sidekick.

"What's the damage?" asks Sheldon.

"There's no time to lose. Who else is playing tonight?"

"I don't know. Why?"

"Because that's how long we've got DiMaggio." My captor's already tapping the screen of his black rectangular apparatus. "We've got to make it count."

Everything's like it was before, with one key difference: they're in high stress mode. They fret, squabble, and sweat. It's clear they want to win as much soiled green paper as they can before the magic—meow!—disappears. I don't know what they're both so excited for.

After all, who's the soothsayer here?

I can't see how it will all work out, only that it will. My mind is fuzzy. Maybe they lulled me into complacency with their fresh tuna, superficial affection, and all that catnip. Perhaps I imagined that, by helping them win green paper, I could ingratiate myself to them, and they'd have mercy on me and set me free. It's possible I let it all go to my head.

But the future is now, and I won't let it slip through my grasp.

When they set out the bowls (filled in a nervous, sloppy rush), I feign disinterest, forcing them to coax and cajole me. At my leisure, I approach my dishes and sniff suspiciously at their contents. "Come on, DiMaggio," they say, "we're in a hurry." So I take my time. They ask me their questions—this team or that one, over or under—ad nauseam. How could there be so many in one day? I'm drawn to the winners every time by this force pulsing inside me and filling the air like static during a storm. So it takes focused willpower to choose the losers. Or instead to choose "over" when it should be "under" and vice versa. (What does that even mean?) I'm only giving them what they both deserve.

Usually, Sheldon lures me up onto the couch during the game, where I nestle in beside him for a time so he can scratch behind my ears. But there's none of that today. So I lurk in their peripheral vision.

The glowing box flickers and lurches as my captor jumps from one incomprehensible game to the next. It makes me dizzy. I try to clear my mind; I try to focus. But that fuzziness remains. I think: difference. I think: distance. I think: sushi. The glowing box flashes, and the sound changes quality.

"What the?" says Sheldon.

"I don't know," my captor explains. "It's stuck."

He turns it off; he turns it on. Nothing helps.

Sheldon grunts. "So we've got, what? The Tokyo Giants?"

"Looks like it," says my captor. "What do they call it? Besuboru."

"We've got to see the end of these games, Farnsie."

"What about Deuces?"

"That sports bar on Sunset?" Sheldon asks.

"They'll at least have a couple on, right?"

The sidekick grabs his jacket and an aluminum cylinder from the box of ice. "Okay, Farnsie. Let's go."

I meander back to the bedroom and fall asleep on top of the blanket. I dream I'm dressed in a brightly colored uniform. I'm on a strangely shaped field of dirt and chalk and grass, and thousands of people smile and shout with anticipation. I can't understand what they're saying. My name is called over the loudspeaker and applause surges. There are sticks and balls. People scattered across the field wear gloves on their hands. Everyone seems to be staring at me, watching and waiting.

I'm roused by the creaking door. Groggy, I listen as my captor throws all six locks, and he and his sidekick shuffle around the apartment. Neither says much. I scamper out to the living room, hoping I'll know what to do when the time comes.

"There's the little bastard," says my captor.

"It's not DiMaggio's fault, Farnsie."

"Then whose is it?"

"We broke the pattern." Sheldon clears his throat. "When we only bet on the Giants, we couldn't lose. But we broke the pattern. That's the way the cookie crumbles."

"So now what?" my captor asks.

"Now we hear from the bookie."

"Who?"

"Where've you been? That's how it works," Sheldon says.

A few minutes later, my captor's black rectangular apparatus starts singing.

"There he is," says Sheldon.

"This isn't happening."

"We're fucked, Farnsie. We've got to come up with a plan."

It's midmorning, and I lounge in the sun, relaxed but alert. My captor and his sidekick sit around and sweat; in fact, the whole place stinks of fear and something dank I can't identify. My captor lets his black rectangular apparatus sing and sing, like a canary in a cage.

The sun has begun to set when someone thumps on the door.

"Open the fucking door, Sheldon."

My captor takes a few steps that direction. "Sorry, no one here by that name."

"Want me to call my boys? Or can we handle this like gentlemen?"

I spring down from the window and skulk beneath the papasan chair.

My captor unfastens all the locks but the chain. I sneak over and sit next to the floor lamp.

"You must be Farnsworth," says the bookie. "Open the door before I kick it in."

My captor does as he's told. The bookie steps into the room and fills the doorway. He's draped in a black jacket, and reflective sunglasses, and he carries a long, tapered stick.

"So what happened, fellas?" he says.

My captor stares at the scuffed parquet. The sidekick wheezes.

"Okay, I'll tell you. You got fucking greedy, is what." The bookie scans the room. "But you've been good customers, so I won't break your legs. All I need's the vig."

"The what?" says Farnsworth.

"The vigorish," Sheldon explains.

For an instant, I think he says, "Licorice," and my heart jumps.

"My cut," the bookie says. "Good faith and all."

I have no idea what they're talking about.

"We don't have it," says Sheldon. "But we'll give you what we can."

"What you got?"

Sheldon begins to stammer. "Not much since my ex cleaned me out last year. A fifty-dollar watch, a monthly bus pass, eight bucks in cash. Plus, Farnsworth's phone."

My captor steals into the kitchen and returns with the grubby shoebox. He flips the lid off and passes it to the bookie.

"Least it's something," says the bookie, stuffing the roll of green paper in his pocket. "But that ain't gonna cut it, fellas. Not even close."

A dirty silence fills the room.

Then my captor blurts: "DiMaggio."

"What?" says the bookie.

"What?" says Sheldon.

"DiMaggio," Farnsworth repeats. "My cat. She has powers. She can tell the future."

The bookie grins. "Like a fortuneteller, you mean?"

"Don't do this," says Sheldon.

"You gotta be shittin me," the bookie says. "Can he talk, too?"

"She," says Sheldon.

My captor shakes his head. "No, it's true. How do you think we won so much?"

"Last I checked, you were in the hole. Deep."

"She's clairvoyant."

"Clair what?" The bookie glances at me and smiles. "Anyway I got pit bulls. They'd eat that thing alive."

I must be distracted by the mention of dogs, because my captor scoops me up before I can bound to safety. I wiggle and squirm, but he clutches me with a strength I never suspected he had. Then he tries to foist me on the man in the black jacket.

"I don't want your goddamn gypsy cat," says the bookie. "But you have something for me by the end of the day tomorrow. Maybe your car? What do you drive?" No one says a word. "Or I won't waste anybody's time sending my boys. I'll sick the pit bulls on you instead."

I twist and wriggle in my captor's grasp until I wrench my forepaws free. Then out come the claws. A swipe, then two more, deep enough to draw blood. Farnsworth shouts and drops me. Sheldon makes a grab for me and misses. Then the bookie tries to block my way, but I feint right and go left. Now I dash down the hallway. I'm down the stairs in two quick leaps, then around the corner and out the door.

Freedom!

Outside, traffic swells on the boulevard. Once I'm a safe distance from my captor, I prance and scamper in the cool evening air that smells of salt and cypress and steamed rice. In the near distance, waves lap at the beach. The last rays of sunlight shimmer through a thin blanket of evening fog. Several unseen canines, chained to stakes or locked in crates, catch my scent and begin to bay. I think: poor suckers. I think: gorgeous evening. I think: Lisa will be here soon. I shouldn't stray too far; I don't want to worry her. So I slip into the shadows to wait, grinning as the first stars flicker into focus.

PROCYON LOTOR

Ariana-Sophia Kartsonis

Ray shuffles ahead of me, his bag dragging so that it rolls against the ground and the apples became more like ball-bearings than crisp planets. Ray's wide back moves saturated in moonlight, as if some of the light had soaked in and a silverness glows off him. His hands, like mine, are leathery-slender-stars: likely aching from the grip. Less and less often now, we linger with what we find. We scuffle off into the blue-blackness, away from those that would do us harm. The cold is a winding, bone-finding kind and nothing that cloaks us is adequate. Too much time in the laboratory has changed the climate for us.

A dry leaf's whisper across a shoe, we are stealthy, agile, silent. I know these things from watching. When you're mostly made of fear and secret, you watch closely. When you watch closely, there are things subtler than most would guess. One season leans against another, making difficult the task of discerning one from the other. But if your life depends on it, you learn to notice shifts in the tree-trunk and shadow-drunk field.

Our days-before had been manmade and our schedule that of those who studied us. Our world-before had corners and walls. When we broke from it, we broke into new climates, a floor that ran far, far ahead of our elegant feet, and a ceiling that never stopped, only rolled and unraveled.

We memorized locks. It wasn't their machinations that captured our interest, it was that they could keep things from us. We liked best those galaxies we could pry open. *Let there be nothing locked away from our inspection, Connie*, Ray used to say. He meant: let nothing ever fall lost on us.

Nothing did. So that it took only a hot day when the windows had been opened. The fall of night when we noticed the latch was not fully engaged. With our fabulous hands, their penchant for recalling that the new locks were old tricks to us, we pushed open the grid. Before we made our escape, our bodies dreamed these climbable places, our arms ached to pull us into a tree's hold, even before we'd touch our first branch. Our bodies knew such a thing to long for; they ached to reach that unmade memory.

In the beginning the boundlessness of it left us clinging to the edges of things. The muggy late-summer sky stuck to our bodies. Trees cradled us as we found our rhythm, astonished by the first snap of true winter. By then, we walked in the open—a dark kettle of midnight and beyond—and the branches gridding the horizon brought back the graph-paper-view of our lives before. We stopped clinging to walls and embankments, left ditches to search for the easy meals of what others discarded. If our past life had been devoted involuntarily to the advancement of science, our new life was the science of re-discovering instinct.

Parks and playgrounds offer us shelter but also a life span less than one-tenth of the one before, and our food is pilfered instead of offered to us: the bag of apples filched from the campsite: we devour them.

What if we'd stayed? Stayed until we outlived our usefulness as subject and data? Though able to indicate which light bulb amongst a panel of bulbs had been lit—a full twenty-five seconds after it dimmed—even as we rifled through the pockets of lab assistants before giving them our full attention, we'd never been particularly able to shed our stubborn autonomy. In time, more pliant subjects would be found. What if we'd never left and, instead of being destroyed, we lived nearly twenty years in some zoo or any climate-controlled habitat, free of cars and those that wish to end the overly-curious? These days, Ray and I will be lucky to pull down a full year. At the edge of a freshly mowed lawn, we pull the lid off a garbage can and listen hard.

Get away from that. It's ours!

Terrified, we watch, immigrants to the kingdom of our species. Our gaze, unlike the deer's frantic fleeing, is read as a challenge.

Whatever else this "ours" is, it's all things. Cities and woods, buildings, water, food, sky, air. We wander further and they take that further, too. No place a place for our keeping. So we live in their margins. Ray and me, two more quickly-drawn beings trying to skirt their infinite expansions, the scrawls and scribbles of their widening range, for any place to live.

How we know what we know now is beyond us. The human things and the nocturnal, garbage-rifling dinnertime of our life-after confound us. There is only smell, touch, and the memory of all there is that we can't do for the others, those fallen-us left behind, their shapes left for days on the highway, so that sometimes we only know them as our own by the tails on the asphalt, moving with the wind. There they wave like ringed flags from a country that is only wilderness, struggle, the night's forgiving middle-hours, and our charged, silent travels through the indifferent air.

RED ADMIRAL

Jonathan Balcombe

As a boy of six I found a large, freshly dead beetle on a family trip to the beach. Its beauty for me was infinite: metallic light green color, a perfect white spot on each elytron, and flawless symmetry. I prized it and kept it for days until my mother, tiring of its rank odor, had me bury it in the yard. A year later I plucked a drowned cicada from a puddle. I already knew cicadas lived underground for years before emerging as adults; I admired their brown husks clinging to tree trunks in mid-summer like tiny tanks emerged from a subterranean military world. I took my cicada home and left it on my bedroom desktop. When I returned from school the next day, I discovered my tank risen from the dead, inching across the desk, leaving a trail of water in her wake. The god of insects was reimbursing me for my lost beetle.

I had an uncle who collected insects as a hobby. I gazed with horrified fascination at his specimens, carefully arrayed in rank and file, lifeless. He saw and nurtured my interest. My innocence hardened; by age eleven I was pinning moths to cork boards. In eighth grade I made a large drawing of a scorpion fly I'd found dead on the front porch. I spent a week meticulously recording in pencil every hair and wing vein. Two years later, my project on the taxonomy of a subfamily of weevils from Eastern Ohio won a regional science fair, and culminated in a new species that bears my name: *Otiorrhynchus samfordi*.

I never married. At twenty-five, I had an assistant professorship at a private college. I collected with abandon, published dozens of papers in obscure taxonomy journals, secured enough grants to keep the promotions and tenure committee happy, and presented my work at conferences. I had occasional short-term relationships but they meant little more than a sense of validation—reassurance that I was not a robot. My days were otherwise patterned, structured. I drank tea obsessively, adored Bach, scheduled all my meals and worked monk-like every morning, weekends included.

It was a term assignment that brought Vanessa to my office. It was thirty years on, and by that time, my academic life was in decline. I collected sporadically, and then mostly vicariously through the efforts of graduate students who I sent into the field with pitfall traps. My hours at the dissecting microscope diminished. The parade of dead beetles grew musty. Each student was to collect a local insect and describe its life history. In addition to behavioral observations, I wanted a mounted specimen.

"Dr. Samford," she said, "I don't want to kill my insect. Will you accept a photograph instead?"

Though it didn't sound like a request, her directness belied her posture: she sat slightly hunched, hands clasped in her lap, her straight red hair tied in a ponytail.

"But a photograph is a two-dimensional representation of three dimensions, a shadow of the real thing," I replied.

"As is a dead insect compared to a living one," she said.

I looked at her, wary of the implication. "You realize that the idea that insects are sentient is ridiculous, don't you? There isn't enough neural tissue to support conscious experience in an insect."

"But according to last week's readings, paper wasps recognize the facial features of other colony members, and honey bees can learn to discriminate between images of human faces."

"It's good to meet a student who appreciates the reading assignments."

"Well, it sounds pretty conscious to me."

"It's just one insect. There are countless more to replace it. Do you know that a single fruit fly can spawn generations of flies? By year's end, they could amass in a dense ball that would reach the diameter of the sun."

A small turquoise stud nestled against each of her earlobes. I noticed the subtle rise and fall of her chest beneath her cream cardigan.

"Yes, I read that in the opening chapter of our textbook. It's amazing, but it seems irrelevant." She paused, then added: "Please, I'm a straight-A student in my final year. I love this course and I adore insects. I don't want to harm them."

My resolve was ebbing. I decided to change the subject. "Did you know the genus of the red admiral butterfly is Vanessa? Admirals are palatable, but experienced birds leave them alone because they look like their toxic, bad-tasting cousins, the monarchs."

Vanessa played her gambit: "Well, if you want to be left alone, let me photograph my specimen for the term assignment."

"If I let you submit a photograph, other students will want to follow suit."

"I hope so," she said. "It's more insects spared the pin and cork board."

"Then I want a series of photographs showing dorsal, ventral, lateral, frontal, and caudal aspects."

"Consider it done. Thank you, Dr. Samford."

She rose to go. I stood and offered my hand. She shook it with a firm grip. I decided that I liked this butterfly.

I didn't expect I'd see her in my office again. I was wrong. A week later she was back. She wanted to know why I studied beetles, if their diversity fascinated me. I recalled that the early twentieth century British evolutionary biologist JBS Haldane was once asked what might be inferred about God's view of creation from the works of nature. He is reputed to have replied, "An inordinate fondness for beetles."

She thought about this for a moment. "Do you think that someday insects will inherit the world?"

"That's anthropocentric, don't you think? Assuming you believe humans own it now."

She blinked and looked out the window. "Well, we act like we run the show. But we seem to have an unprecedented capacity to soil our own nest."

I couldn't help chuckling at that. "If you want my opinion, insects inherited the world long ago, and they're not giving it up anytime soon."

Her gaze remained fixed on the window, but I could detect a smile.

"And you're dead right about humans. We're a house of cards waiting to fall. Genetic change is slow to take hold in humans, whereas the nimble genes of insects are recombining every few weeks. Fruit flies have 500 generations to our one. Millions of years after the last human is gone from the Earth, a cockroach will be relaxing on a leaf, preening its antennae."

Vanessa visited my office every week for the remainder of the term. We discussed mostly insects, life on Earth, and a deeply shared cynicism for our own species. But whereas my cynicism was steeped in negativity and denial, hers percolated with optimism and hope. Her term assignment featured a series of exquisite macro photographs of a ground beetle, *Carabus nemoralis*, with detailed descriptions of its behavior:

> Because they are so small and easily crushed, insects symbolize the most abusable and malignable of life forms. Though they are inexorable and dominant in their numbers, individually they are vulnerable. If we can acknowledge the integrity of the individual insect, then we can acknowledge that of all other sentient life forms.

I was smitten.

One night, I worked late tallying final-term grades and bumped into Vanessa on the way to my car. I offered her a lift and we drove to her off-campus apartment. She invited me in for a cup of tea. She put on the *Goldberg Variations*, Glenn Gould's last recording. There was a bottle of gin. We talked and laughed. But I didn't let myself go: she remained a butterfly of my memory, a photograph, a shadow.

I saw her only once afterwards. I believe she graduated the following spring.

I immersed myself back into my work. I collected beetles and I pinned them. I published like I had in my thirties. In time, I was once again the aging professor—a veneer of propriety and industriousness. But it didn't last.

Six years on, I emerged again. At an entomology conference in Mexico, following the morning plenary, I found myself relaxing at the deserted hotel swimming pool among lush shade trees and blooming hibiscus bushes. I settled into a deck chair and dangled my right foot into the water. The undulating wheeze of cicadas cleaved the air. A column of leafcutter ants scurried along its well-worn path through a nearby patch of grass.

I noticed a long, slender grasshopper floating nearby. I rose and scooped the insect up with my hand. I put on my reading glasses. A tiny beetle was clinging to one of its antennae like a sailor riding a storm-tossed ship's mast. It was scarcely bigger than a pinhead, but unmistakably coleopteran. It walked to the tip of the antenna, which bent slightly under its weight. Waving its own antennae, the beetle raised its elytra, unsheathed its wings, and flew off.

I thought of Vanessa. I thought of all the beetles I had destroyed during my career. I saw legs waving helplessly as

I plopped their owners into ether jars. With rising nausea, I wondered how many young minds I had corrupted with the notion that the creatures were put here for us? "You bastard," I muttered before looking furtively about, realizing I'd said it aloud.

That night I dreamt I was at the cinema, watching a propaganda film, developed to foment some sort of political antipathy. Titled *Swat*, it depicted the moment of impact of a fly swatter on an ordinary housefly. Glued to a tabletop, the fly's destruction was captured by an ultra-high-speed camera mounted three inches away. One second stretched out to three minutes. As the fly swatter gradually descended towards the fly, the fly's escape response triggered and the wings sprung into action. Gossamer membranes waved gracefully, glinting blue and silver under the lights. The legs extended, but the fly was trapped. The shadow darkened. On impact, the fly disintegrated in excruciating detail. The head deformed, fluids squirted from shattering eye facets, innards gushed from tracheal tubes. The animal was already dead before its body met the tabletop, where it was flattened—a wet wafer doing a final pirouette as the swatter withdrew.

The audience members stood and cheered loudly. I sat there, chalk faced and blank.

I woke to an exquisite sky. I skipped the last day of the conference and spent four hours fishing insects from the swimming pool. Some were fully alive, flying from my hand or crawling onto an offered leaf. Others were quite dead and never stirred from where I placed them. Most, however, turned out to be like my cicada: inert when I retrieved and examined them, but the ember of life still glowing within. I watched with great satisfaction as this wasp's or that beetle's wings began to twitch and buzz. When I left the poolside, several dozen tiny beings had either taken wing or were readying themselves to do so.

ONE OF YOUR NUMBER

Diane Josefowicz

Once my name was Bertram Outram, and I was not an orphan.

What I am is a striped-face capuchin monkey, *Cebus lotoricus*, commonly known as the raccoon capuchin, and I have lived, if this attenuated existence can be called "living," in Habitat One for just under a year.

I am not what I was. We are not what we were.

In addition to a mother and a father, before coming to Habitat One I had an assortment of aunts and uncles, and a grandmother so dexterous she could make Brazil nuts appear from behind my ears whenever I was unhappy. But I was seldom unhappy. I was the seventh of fifteen siblings, the twelfth of twenty-two cousins, the stalwart middle of our troop.

Although the range of the striped-face capuchin is presently limited to the Amazon Basin, at one time we could be found throughout the tropical isotherm of the New World. An activist clutch of *H. taxonomicus* split us off from the branches of our extended family—the elegant red-hatted branch, the plump golden-bellied branch, the demure tiny-eared branch—severely limiting our numbers on paper. Worse than the depredations of *H. taxonomicus*, however, have been the incursions of *H. economicus*—with their river-damming, clear-cutting, and, not least, fire-setting, which they accomplished by arcing their spent cigarettes, still lit, into the air, which is no longer quite wet enough to extinguish them.

It happened one night after bedtime, when I was scooped from my nest in the crotch of a quebracho and flung through the darkness into the echoing rear of a metal conveyance. My family had scattered. Why I alone was chosen, I do not know. Perhaps my sleep was deeper; perhaps my family could not warn me; perhaps they did not try. The man who captured me stank like a cougar. Since then, this same man has been entrusted with my care at Habitat One. From my observations, I have concluded that he is an example of neither *H. economicus* (they smell like cigarettes and cash) nor *H. taxonomicus* (they don't smell like anything) but of some entirely different species. His name tag says Zookeeper.

Here is my problem: The Zookeeper, who is as dim a bulb as any devised by *H. economicus*, does not understand that I am a striped-face capuchin monkey. Rather, he thinks I am a flag-tailed pongo raccoon. I should add that there are no monkeys here to speak of, unless you count the stuffed ones, the Monkeez Paloosh™ available for sale in the Habitat One Boutique. And although there *is* a colony of flag-tailed pongo raccoons here in Habitat One, I am not one of their number. First of all, I do not look anything like a flag-tailed pongo raccoon. I do not have their round, importunate eyes, nor their weak if impressively bushy tails, nor their agouti markings, which leave me cold but are no doubt quite lovely to those of their sort. Nor, it must be said, do I have their complaisant stupidity. In this, they resemble the Zookeeper, which is probably why their colony has been given over to his care, like attracting like here in Habitat One as it does anywhere else in the animal kingdom. What *I* am, however, is a striped-face capuchin monkey. Like others of my number, and unlike flag-tailed pongo raccoons, I am diurnal and arboreal, with opposable thumbs, reflective self-awareness, and an incredibly long and muscular tail, if I may say so myself.

Which I may, for now at least.

The Zookeeper's efforts to induct me into the society of flag-tailed pongo raccoons have been incessant, and in this regard wholly typical of the activities of others of his relentless number. There is, I admit, a mulish charm in his persistence. He scatters within my reach numerous small objects beloved by flag-tailed pongo raccoons: lengths of tinsel, rancid sandwiches, bits of reflective tape. Once he left a trap: a dozen bamboo skewers, much beloved of the raccoons who, when extremely bored, use them to dig ants from anthills, a behavior that invariably causes the Zookeeper to scrawl some banality on his clipboard, e.g., *Tool use!* Needless to say, I am not so dumb as to fall for that. His efforts have only demonstrated his limitless ignorance of the habits and preferences of capuchin monkeys. At home our traffic in shiny objects is limited to using them as a medium for exchange—we have this much in common with *H. economicus.* Unlike raccoons, we are fussy omnivores with a taste for soft fruits like mangoes and bananas. Alas, when it comes to food I regret to say that here on Habitat One my diet has been limited to what I can scavenge when the Zookeeper departs for his evening meal—a few acorns, a lemon wedge, rose hips from the patch I discovered one day near the southern edge of the shade cast by the copper beech in whose limbs I spend most of my time. When the Zookeeper left me half his lunch, wrapped in wax paper and deposited at the base of the beech, I regret that I was sorely tempted.

"Come down," he coos at me, in the same tones of frantic mollification that he uses to coax the witless raccoons from heating vents, overturned pails, and the numberless other tight spaces in which they are forever enclosing themselves. "Come down little flag-tailed pongo raccoon."

I chitter in reply, to be polite, but I stay where I am. If we are resolute, we capuchin monkeys, no one could say that we are not well-mannered. Whereas the raccoons are silent and come when he warbles, like dogs. But even in this I cannot credit them with *politesse*. Like dogs, they seem to have no choice.

He taunts me. First, a new raccoon, female, was added to the colony, without a corresponding male. When I ignored her, she was attacked so ferociously by the other females that another male had to be brought in to placate them. I threw my feces in, too, to make things more interesting—*politesse* being, as ever, the first casualty of confinement. After the failure of that effort to lure me into the raccoon colony, the Zookeeper released lactating male bats near the copper beech. They hung upside down from the branches, their babies hanging upside-down also, clutching their fathers' chests, their mouths latched firmly to the paternal nipple, while the mothers fed the fathers revolting scraps from the raccoons' trough. When the lactating bats failed to put me sufficiently in mind of fatherhood, and further throwing of feces had no appreciable effect, the Zookeeper left dozens of slipper snails on a stump on the north side of the copper beech. In an hour, they had formed silvery piles from which the Zookeeper removed the bottom-most, always female, after which the new bottom-most member would turn from male to female. What was the Zookeeper trying to suggest? Insulted, I retreated deeper into the branches of the copper beech and did not chitter again when he could hear. I did throw a final piece of shit at him but, truth be told, without my usual enthusiasm. He can't figure out what I am, but somehow he understands how much I would like a companion, even a family, if such a thing is still possible for me. How can that imbecile know anything?

It is well you should ask. The problem began, I believe, when various instances of *H. taxonomicus* addressed themselves to the vexed issue of what to call those of my number. This problem, initially limited to nomenclature, has since ramified, becoming specific, concrete, and for me, *personal*. Solving the Zookeeper's problem with my identity now takes up virtually my entire existence. If I may be permitted a theoretical note: The great solace of names is that they are particular. The right name says: *I am this, and none other*. Names carve the world of ideas, separating an idea of *this* from another idea, of *that*, creating boundaries which, if sustained, can hold all sorts of things—anger, hatred, devouring love. Put another way: A robust nomenclature keeps the papaya salad away from the slipper snail casserole, so nobody gets a headache. Yet here on Habitat One, something has gone taxonomically wrong. It is as if the Zookeeper's name for flag-tailed pongo raccoon also contained the name for capuchin monkey, as if the Zookeeper's definition of "flag-tailed pongo raccoon" were overinclusive in just this way. That, at any rate, is the best explanation I have been able to come up with.

I hang upside-down at the furthest edge of the longest southern branch of the giant copper beech, so close I can smell the raccoons' leftovers and their rancid agouti fur. The Zookeeper has installed a hut nearby, the better, I suppose, to keep watch on the raccoon enclosure. The population has recently undergone an alarming expansion, for the females have all had their litters. They keep close to their babies the whole day and night, a habit of attention that I believe is greatly reassuring to the Zookeeper who, as a great devotee of the anodyne waking dream known as basic cable television, is occupied with his favorite programs for long stretches of the day. His most beloved is a half-hour cooking show featuring a well-nourished woman with a glossy brown pelt and a flair for speedy meal preparation, although the Zookeeper's attraction to her might also just stem from her large brown eyes—which look remarkably like those of a pongo raccoon! At the end of each show, as she lays out platters of food she has cooked, she smiles invitingly before taking a bite of everything herself, to show that all is good and safe to eat. The Zookeeper looks on, agog, swallowing mightily. I regret to report that I've grown somewhat fond of her as well. If she were real, she might have my heart. I think she must have the Zookeeper's.

Oblivious to the Zookeeper's preoccupation, not to mention my presence on the copper beech, one of the new mothers waddles across the enclosure, her children hanging precariously off her midsection like frightened rowers clinging to their capsized boat. She collapses into her nest, a box filled with shredded newspaper, none too clean, where the babies root in her fur. Their tender pink skin still shines beneath their downy new coats. It is a scene to warm your heart, if it doesn't first turn your stomach: the squeaking and the smells and the dopey contentment of the mother, enjoying the sun bright on her pointed face, her agouti fur, her ridiculous, full-fed, contented, malodorous babies. I hate them, *all* of them. Worse, I hate myself. Hatred is a feeling, and a feeling implies a relationship. But if there is one thing I know with complete authority, it is that there is no relationship. There is nothing, *nothing*, between them and me. I am not one of their number.

I do understand that, from a certain point of view, all my troubles would disappear if only I would accept the position that has been created "for" me in the raccoon colony. But some days I am so wound up with frustration—with the dim-witted Zookeeper, the equally dumb raccoons, in short, the whole idiotic situation—that even feces-flinging provides no relief. In those circumstances I have no choice but to withdraw to the giant copper beech, climb to the highest branch, and screech at the top of my voice. Of course, nothing changes as a result of this exercise. The hawk circles as usual above my head; my stomach signifies its emptiness; the summer heat continues to oppress Habitat One. No one is any smarter or any more aware of my existence, which has dwindled to the single fact of my not being a pongo raccoon but a striped-face, chittering, gesticulating, feces-throwing capuchin MONKEY with an empty stomach and, may I add, again and for the record, an immensely long and muscular tail. Agh! I could scream. So I do. I do. For ten or fifteen minutes, my screaming breaks the stillness of Habitat One. The stillness continues, nothing changes at all. But sometimes I feel just a little bit better.

Some weeks after my arrival on Habitat One, I discover at the southernmost tip of southernmost branch of the giant copper beech a crescent-shaped blue lake that stretches for at least a half mile in either direction. On the opposite shore, the lake is garlanded with additional copper beeches; above them rises a mountain topped with snow. The overall effect is that of an excessively picturesque postcard, the sort that exists only to inspire envy in the receiver: *I am here. Don't you wish you were, too?* Everything changes, however, after sunset, when the darkness hides the copper beeches, with their imposing size and disconcerting loveliness (nothing so large should be so pretty), and the stars regard themselves icily in the mirror of the lake. At these times, fully in the grip of an atmospheric sublimity not amenable to capture on ordinary picture postcards, I scramble along the southernmost branch of the copper beech until I nearly reach the tip, whereupon, propelling myself with immensely long and muscular tail, I catapult myself into the air, end over end over end. My parabola arcs and diminishes. I splash into the lake, and the geese scatter, honking.

In addition to the idiocy she shares with the rest of her species, the newest raccoon mother, my intended paramour, suffers the inexperience of youth. This is her first litter. It may well be her last. She leaves the babies alone for minutes at a time while she cavorts in the haystack with a raccoon that may very well be her brother, though it is hard to say, for they all look alike. Once the hawk flew over Habitat One, circled the raccoon enclosure, and put the nest in its shadow. I was sure all three babies were goners.

One morning, I woke to screams. The young mother wailed as she scurried in wide circles around the pen, circles that narrowed as she screamed louder, closing in on her nest which now had only two babies in it. I crawled out on the copper beech limb as far as I could, not wanting to watch and not wanting to miss anything either. She calmed down when the Zookeeper fed her a sedative secreted in a rind. As he did, I hung from my tail with pains in my gut, sick with the smell of blood in my fur. How long before he figured it out? A bad wind blew from the MadCatz! exhibit, but for once I did not plug my nose. I swung far above the raccoons and the Zookeeper, as they mourned the loss of one of their own.

One night, leaping from the giant copper beech, I am astonished to discover someone else, someone *new*, beside me, as I fly through the air. She is not yet more than a whirl of fur, but even so, I am filled with a wonderful, unfamiliar feeling. In the moonlight, I can't be sure, but I think she might be one of our number!

This goes on for some nights but I never catch more than a glimpse of her—opposable thumbs, an adorable haunch, eyes that flash with intelligence as we swing through the dark.

Roaming by the lake, I pluck American Beauties one by one, picking off their petals and eating the sour hips.

"Stop it," someone says. A female voice. I am in the middle of my fourth American Beauty, but the voice is so commanding I drop it at once. "Those are mine."

She sidles toward me through the high grass. The curve of her haunch is unmistakable. It is my night-flying friend, who by her markings really does appear, in full daylight, to be a striped-face capuchin monkey.

"You are one of our number," I observe, full of wonder.

"You are eating my babies." A sentence like a shove. I must have looked alarmed because she added, "Not literal babies. But you have to understand that I've been growing these since last year, and after all the work I've done I would prefer that you didn't make a snack out of them."

"I'm sorry." I mean it. Her sadness at the loss of her roses has vanquished my hunger more effectively than any food. "I've been so hungry."

I am so diminished my hip bones stick out from my lower back. But my friend looks well-nourished, sleek, lightly padded. How ever does she manage it? She gives me a long look.

"It's all right. You didn't eat many."

"I only ate *one* baby flag-tailed pongo raccoon!"

Her eyes widen. My stomach rolls; too many rose hips, too many baby raccoons.

"And it made me very sick, too!"

She touches my hand.

"You were provoked," she soothes me. "And like you said, hungry."

She encloses me in her sleek arms, and I sob for a long time. Anyone can be provoked to anything at all, when he is hungry.

"Let's stick to nuts and berries from now on," she says, when I am done crying.

She leads me to the southernmost branch of the copper beech. Even though it is broad daylight, we fling ourselves into the lake, end over end over end.

When we're too tired to swim anymore, we rest in the shade of the copper beech. The breeze ruffles my hair. She shifts, the better to take me in. There is no judgment in the look. I have nothing to fear, and yet, my breathing comes in urgent spurts. Should I ask her? Do I dare?

"Do I look like a raccoon to you?"

She frowns. "What's a raccoon?"

After that, my whole strategy changed. Instead of throwing feces at the Zookeeper, instead of chattering and gesticulating in my language, I wondered how I might begin to speak his. How could I actually *convince* the Zookeeper that I was not a flag-tailed pongo raccoon but a striped-face capuchin monkey?

The Zookeeper, I observed, reasoned according to similarities. Pongo raccoons went in the enclosure devoted to pongo raccoons; old food from the raccoons' trough went in the trash with the Zookeeper's uneaten lunch. Perhaps my striped face reminded him of a pongo raccoon, and that association was the source of his error. To rectify it would require the establishment of a different order of likeness in his mind— that I was far *more* like a monkey than a pongo raccoon.

But there were no monkeys around with which to compare myself, except for my friend, whose existence I did not wish to betray. As she did not have my long experience with the Zookeeper, I feared for her safety, and my own.

There were, however, the Monkeez Paloosh™ in the Habitat One Boutique. In the end it did not prove difficult to steal one of their number. There had to have been thirty piled beside the door near the killer whale display, and the woman who worked the cash register had left to answer the staff telephone. At the last moment, I hesitated, wondering which to take. Each wore the same small red cap (much like my distant relatives in the red-capped part of my family) and an alarming fixed leer. I admit the leer nearly did me in. Was it hungry, or murderous, or plain stupid? No time to decide. At the back of the shop, the cashier was ending her call. I grabbed the nearest *M. paloosh* and fled.

I returned to the copper beech and left the stuffed monkey by the raccoon enclosure. My hope was that the Zookeeper, upon finding it, would come to an insight: *Bertram Outram is not a raccoon but a monkey!* I did not hope, at this point, that he would recognize anything more specific about me—not my species, not my sentience, certainly not my immensely long and muscular tail. Six months in Habitat One had taught me to lower my expectations.

I went to the lake, hoping to meet my friend, but I did not find her that day, or on any of the other days that followed. The rose bushes were still there, in excellent condition, looking as if no one had ever popped off even a single hip. On the ground I discovered a desiccated monkey dropping with a smell that seemed familiar. I prodded it with a stick (tool use!), but its fragments yielded nothing, not even a single undigested rose pip.

Means nothing, I consoled myself. Circumstantial evidence is no evidence at all.

At which point Habitat One went completely silent: not a peep from the Bird Cage, not a meow from MadCatz! I caught a whiff of stagnant water, then the peculiar smell that electricity trails as it leaps through the air. The ground beneath me split with a stupendous noise. I clapped my hands over my ears, leapt to the far side of the widening gap, and sprinted back to the safety of the copper beech, where I mashed my face into the trunk and clung to it for what felt like hours.

The trembling ceased; the air cooled; the afternoon, as usual, subsided. Bewildered, I made my way, swinging from paw to paw, to a higher crotch of the copper beech, where I could observe the Zookeeper's hut and the raccoon enclosure. I expected to find some evidence of the disturbance and even, I admit, half-hoping for it. But nothing had changed. The babies were asleep with their mothers; the remains of their swill stank in the trough; the Zookeeper's television transmitted pictures of the brown-eyed lady who smilingly ladled steaming soup into mugs that she topped with bread and cheese. As ever, once her preparations were finished she offered the melange to the camera, as if to say that, no matter how bad things got out there, those of her number would not only manage to keep the lid on their seething, but also derive some gooey benefit from it. A home truth, a bit of kitchen wisdom.

It was then that I realized: *M. paloosh* was missing.

A scrabbling from the raccoon enclosure caught my attention. *M. paloosh* sneered at me from within the baby raccoons' nest. For once the babies were quiet, intensely occupied by their efforts, largely successful, to remove his stuffing through his ears.

I am scheduled for trial, and it is likely that I will be punished. Since I am not allowed to speak, even with the Zookeeper (as if I would), I haven't asked what form this might take. I hear rumors, though. At times, there is a bang from the courtyard. Someone's veins run with fire in a small, sterile room. A deep hole appears in the brown field at the western edge of Habitat One, and the next day the hole is filled and topped with a bloodstained bag. I do not know what end they have devised for me. This mystery is no big deal, however, because of what I have learned, at last, here on Habitat One.

It started as a game I played with myself to pass the time. I would sit in my cell with my eyes shut, trying to make myself one of them, *H. economicus, H. taxonomicus, H. moronicus* (that is, the Zookeeper), by emptying myself of all that I remembered of being as a stripe-faced capuchin monkey. First I learned to be absolutely quiet. This took some time. In this state of absolute silence, which I learned to extend for minutes, then hours, I forced myself to remember everything— my mother and father, my troop of cousins, my nut-cracking prestidigitating grandmother, and then the horrible transition, the feces I threw, the baby raccoon I ate, the Zookeeper's lunch, my theft of *M. paloosh*, the things I screamed from the top of the copper beech, and most painful of all, my lost friend from the lake. I allowed each image to develop fully, like an instant photograph, and then, no matter how much it hurt me, I wrote it down—and forgot it. If the image returned, I allowed it to develop again, and I revised the original until nothing was left of the memory but a series of marks that filled all four walls of my cell.

The day I started on the ceiling, Zookeeper visited with his clipboard.

Tool, he wrote. *Pencil.*

I ignored him, engrossed by the effort to write while suspended, prone and uncomfortably close to the overhead light, with a pencil I'd chewed to almost nothing.

Use: ?

He returned with a notebook and a new yellow pencil topped with a hard nub which might once have been useful for eliminating errors but now only leaves a red smear over whatever I try to obliterate. The only solution is not to make mistakes. This constraint has had a certain effect. If I have written less than I might otherwise, I have done so with more conviction.

To fill the spaces vacated by my memories, I contrive elaborate fantasies of ordinary nonexistence—a small black hole collapsing somewhat trivially upon itself, a misshelved book of no particular importance, a trick of the light on a hot, still day—each of which I pare down to the minimum number of words required for comprehension if not by the Zookeeper, then at least by one of my number. As I do, I learn to think of *myself* as one of these fantasies, which is to say, as a convincingly detailed version of nothing in particular. Let me emend that: nothing *much.* For even "nothing" is too immoderate, too exaggerated, in the end too absolute. My major activity now is simply this process of paring myself down. I am pruning myself, in imagination, to the exact limits of my body. Whatever I am, or have become, I will be exactly one of my number, no more and no less. As I grow thinner—my appetite too has grown ever more abstract, as food has had less and less to do with me—I also grow quieter, more blank, neutral, and indistinct. I can say this much for this activity: It is a discipline, and like any discipline, it orders my existence. It passes the time. In the past several weeks I have improved so much that even the Zookeeper has to look twice, to make sure I really am under the covers at lights-out.

By now what I have become should be clear enough. I am subject to their laws. I have been tried and sentenced for my crimes—theft and murder, yes, but also feces-flinging and disturbing the geese. Tomorrow at dawn the Zookeeper will come for me. I will be brought to a sterile room, or a courtyard, or to the edge of one of their brown fields. Wherever I am, I will quiet myself. I will look my executioner straight in the eye. And then, if I have done everything right, only one thing will be impossible.

A BLINDED HORSE DREAMS OF HIPPOCAMPI

Justin Maxwell

I believe in God.
I believe in mermaids too.
I believe in 72 virgins on a chain. Why not? Why not?
—Nick Cave, "Mermaids"

Characters

THE HORSE: a horse blinded by a stablehand.
THE CHORUS OF SEAHORSES: 60,000 seahorses, played by anywhere between one and 60,000 actors.
THE NIGHTMARE: Is it a horse with flaming hooves, a man with a spike, a wolf in wolf's clothing?

Time

The dreamtime.

Setting

The steppes of a horse's dreamscape.

Nighttime. The stars come out. We are on the vast steppes that all horses dream of. Enter **THE HORSE**, *blind even here. While the* **HORSE** *is speaking,* **THE NIGHTMARE** *enters surreptitiously.*

THE HORSE

Most nights, I can smell the ocean.
The breeze rolls the grass in trochaic breakers,
stress
       lull,
stress
       lull,
stress
       lull,
grain as surf, pollen as flotsam.
The stars sing to the navigators;
the mermaids sing to the sailors;
the seahorses sing to me,
but I am afraid of the hippocampi and their song.
I am afraid of the blurry motion of the world,
of rolling, of closing in,
of the scent of grain breezing over the steppes,
    (realizes **THE NIGHTMARE** *has arrived)*
of the Nightmare, a black horse trimmed in fire.

THE NIGHTMARE

There are things in this world to fear:
the coyote,
the rattlesnake,
the wolf,

the metal spike,
the sudden motion,
the aching void.
Me.

THE HORSE

We do not speak to one another.
The spheres have their music:
we can attempt to listen or we can attempt to ignore.
Any answer would be impotent;
this is no place for dialog.

Better to let the waves wash over me,
pull me down among the hippocampi,
and swim.

Water is the ally of rust;
both are blunting forces.

> *(THE CHORUS OF SEAHORSES enters;*
> *THE NIGHTMARE is unhappy about their*
> *contrapuntal motion.)*

I forgive the spike
I forgive the iron hand,
but I want both to rust away.
I want to be unafraid.

THE CHORUS OF SEAHORSES

Come and see.
Come and see.
    (beat)
The susurrus of the sea is its own song,
our song.
Waves make their own cadence:
wave
    trough
wave
    trough
WAVE.
Three trochaic feet make a line of the ocean's endless epic.
A horse's heart beats a different tattoo;
the sea does not have a mammalian cadence.
Once there was a constellation named Hippocampus;
its stars helped navigators,
and some still hear our songs.
Come and see.
Come and see.

HORSE

There are stars at the bottom of the ocean,
a new way to navigate,
the seahorse,
the hippocampus,
curls deep inside the brain—
in it hums our songs of memory,

>   orientation,
>   trauma.

The hippocampus atrophies with stress,
but still grows new neurons throughout
our lives—
we can always learn trauma.
The seahorse of the ancient Greeks,
is old like starlight:
>   Hippos—horse
>   Kampos—sea monster.

It sings a tempting song.
It is inescapable,
>   submerged in the core of our liquid-electric
>   brains.

A child follows a lullaby into sleep;
a sailor follows the siren to rest on their rocks.
There is no fire underwater
>   just stars
>   and song.

Horses are creatures that follow.

THE NIGHTMARE

Then follow me.
We no longer navigate by the stars:
Bearing dial and a bag of ravens,
chart and sextant,
compass and stopwatch,
radar,

global positioning system.
Eye and light, then
darkness and song.
Always a new way to navigate.
The hippocampus is just part of the brain.
It tells you things too simple to be lies:
I am here,
I was there;
I went from here to there;
I am standing;
I am sitting;
I am prone;
I am wounded;
    I am aching
        It is here
            It is there.

THE HORSE

It is deep in my brain and I
    may know the way
    to, from, away.
To navigate is to follow;
singers sing their songs, and I
follow along.
    (beat)
Or, we follow.
Or, you follow.

THE NIGHTMARE

Only the somnambulist walks into the sea;
do not mistake "dream" for "drown."
There's no devil here,
no god,
no Homer,
no one of deep faith
nor iambic pentameter.

THE HORSE

The vast steppes,
the fathoms of the sea,
the void of space,
are all quiet cradles.
The nightmare descends and becomes
a terrestrial phenomenon.
Perhaps the rocks themselves call
to the sailors,
with sea foam for sirens.
They are justification by sensuality.

Fiery hoof prints scar the sky and evaporate.
The ship's keel groans, cracks, and shatters.
It makes a ship-shaped hole in the surface
of the sea, then it's gone.
All options are disintegration,
and even the good dreams dissipate.
So it is easy to follow,
to listen to the electric song of hippocampi.

THE CHORUS OF SEAHORSES

Come and see
Come and see
Our song is simple.
Our song is succor.
We are the soporific dream of peace.
We are the deep, cool brine.
Come and see.
Come and see.

THE HORSE

Only after I went blind could I hear the hippocampi
call to me.
In the inscrutable stillness
their song comes across the void,
their scree appears, glowing
golden, motes on my useless eyes.
    (beat)
The breeze.
The grain shivers.
My withers tense,
motion in my darkness,
the screen of blindness,
the songs calling me down
into the depth of the sea.

THE CHORUS OF SEAHORSES

Come and see.
Come and see.
    (beat)
Evolution has brought you nothing;
return to the sea.
Brine cleanses,
salt burns away cruelty,
gives scars bioluminescence.
The sea purifies:
liquefies glaciers,
cools magma to archipelagos,
reduces stone to sand,
cliff to beach,
vents energy into the bottom of the ocean,
building fresh worlds in the blind abyss.
Come and see.
Come and see.
    (beat)
Immersion is our future and our past.
Become a glowing star
in our wine-dark sky.
Come and see.
Come and see.

THE HORSE

Better a singer than the song.
Better the unknown cruelty.

Better the aloof fathoms.
Better the indifferent sea.

THE NIGHTMARE

(resentful)
The desiccating sun rises.
The deluging rain descends.
Bacteria grows on the grain.
Mold spores drift on the wind.
There's anthrax in the soil
and tetanus in the rust.
These are the things you know.
Stay with us.

THE HORSE

The spike is in the hand,
the arcing sky,
the clean iron in my eyes
the rusty taste in my mouth.

I too am a singer.
Perhaps you have followed me here?
Perhaps you have heard a song?
Perhaps all songs are the same.
Perhaps I've been a seahorse all along.

Dark. End of play.

CURES AND SUPERSTITIONS

Michael X. Wang

When the package of tiger bones and alligator tails arrived with the monthly shipment of fertilizer, Old Wisdom pasted a neon-green sign in front of his antique and herbal supply store with two words: *They're here!* His son, Ming, had bought the paper in Yuncheng City. Ming had typed up the characters on his computer, blowing up the font and making it blocky. Twenty years old, Ming despised working for his father, who never paid him so much as a penny. Ming had done well in school, top five percent of his class, but only the top two percent got into college. His older brothers had their own families, his mother was dead, and his sister had married out of Xinchun Village to a doctor from Shanghai. Ming was the only one left to tend the fields, his arthritic father in no shape to do anything but package the herbal medicine and man the cash register. To Ming, a popular product like tiger bones simply meant additional labor.

Word of Old Wisdom's shipment traveled fast. By midafternoon, a line spiraled around the store's only aisle and out to the street's bicycle racks. Ming stood next to his father, weighing out grams of ground tiger bones and wrapping them in old editions of *The People's Daily*.

"Mix a pinch of this with a clove of strong ginseng," Old Wisdom told a young woman who was buying the tiger bones for her grandmother. "It won't cure her pain, but it will relieve it for several hours. If you need any ginseng, I have some right here." He motioned for his son to grab a box from the top shelf.

Ming threw the triangular box onto the glass tabletop.

After the woman left, Old Wisdom leaned in to his son, whispering, "You see: mention the other products, make two sales at once."

Ming hated being in the store. The individual products—snakeskin flakes, dried seaweed, and now tiger bones—didn't smell good to begin with, but their odors mixed to create a bitter, vomit-like stench. When he was five years old, he had gotten chickenpox, and his father had brewed him a black, tar-like stew. He hadn't ask his father what was in it, but he remembered it being the most disgusting thing he'd ever tasted, thick as sesame oil and twice as pungent as the bitterest bitter melon. Worst of all, the medicine didn't help; he was sick for over a month. Tigers were nearly extinct. It saddened Ming to think that animals died.

Behind the counter and underneath the ginseng, Old Wisdom was brewing tiger bones with fig leaves in a kettle. He poured it into a ceramic cup, added jasmine tea, and, between customers, took sips.

"You want some?" he asked his son, who shook his head. "It's also great for preventing pain."

To meet demands, Old Wisdom kept the store open until eight, until the summer sun turned red and began to set behind the Blood-cloud Mountains. He was just about to lock the doors and turn off the lights when a car pulled up along the dirt road.

"You caught us just in time," he said, keeping the door open. Then he turned to Ming and shouted, "Don't take away the scale yet. We have another customer."

The man got out of the car—a gleaming black Mercedes—and slammed the door. He wore a striped tie and a dark blue suit left unbuttoned. Walking towards the store with the red sun behind him, he seemed to Old Wisdom like a messiah, like Buddha or Confucius if they had chosen to don modern attire.

Old Wisdom looked at his feet as the man entered. The man scanned the aisle, picking up boxes and then putting them back, on occasion lowering his sunglasses to read a label.

"You have a nice little store here," the man said. "A nice country store."

"Thank you," Old Wisdom said. "What are you looking for? Perhaps I can help."

The man approached the counter. "I'm here in your village to do business, but along the way I thought I'd pick something up for my wife. She's pregnant, you see."

Old Wisdom grew solemn, nodding. "Might I suggest some tiger bones?" He pointed at the pouches on the counter. "It's very fresh; we just got this shipment in today. It's expensive, but I'm sure your wife is worth every penny."

Ming, who had been in the back of the store putting away product, entered carrying a pouch of alligator tails, ready to be separated and sold for tomorrow. It was rare for the store to have customers from the city, and he couldn't help but stare at the man and his nice clothes. The man seemed equally intrigued by Ming. He stared back at the boy, as though stalking prey.

"Is this your son?" the man asked.

"Yes," Old Wisdom said. "This is my son, Ming."

"How old is he?"

"Twenty," said Old Wisdom.

The man reached into his breast pocket and took out a card. "Your son is exactly the type of person I'm looking for." He laid the card on the glass tabletop. "You see, I'm a labor scout. I look for young, strong men from the countryside and bring them to work in the city."

Ming walked over to the counter and picked up the card. On it, there was a name, Zhang Sha, and a position, Director of Search. At the bottom, there was a phone number. Ming didn't recognize the area code.

"I'm not supposed to tell anyone outside of the high school that I'm here, but as soon as I saw your son walk in, I knew he would be interested."

"I'm not sure," Old Wisdom said. "Ming has a bright future in the village."

"Well," said the man, "most likely he won't even beat the odds. With a village this size, there must be a hundred young men who want to leave. We're having an assembly tomorrow."

"What assembly?" Ming asked. "I've never heard of it."

"We like to keep it small. We don't want mobs forming." The man pointed at the tiger bones and told Old Wisdom that he'd like to buy ten grams. Ming weighed out the amount and wrapped it in newspaper. The man lifted the package, bringing it up to his shoulders and then down again. "You sure this is ten grams?" he said. "The scale isn't rigged, is it?"

"No," Old Wisdom said. "Never."

The man smiled. "A joke." He turned to Ming. "If you are interested, be sure to come to your high school tomorrow. The assembly is at five."

After the man left, Old Wisdom scolded his son. "How many times do I have to tell you? When we serve someone from the city, we use the real weights."

On his way to his friend's house, Ming was so excited he rode his bike through a rain puddle, mud splashing onto his pants and ankles. Even though the two of them were the same age, Tao was still in high school. He had been left back twice, and unlike Ming, he never had much hope in escaping the village. The two of them were friends because at one point Ming had liked Tao's sister, who now worked as a flight attendant for Air China.

"The man came to my class," Tao said. "He picked three of us to attend the assembly." Tao was half a foot taller than Ming, and had the habit of craning his neck when speaking.

"Did he tell you how many people he's taking?"

Tao shook his head. "Interviews will be given tomorrow. He told us that, above all, he was looking for people who were capable of enduring hard labor—healthy people."

Nodding, Ming considered the state of his own health. He had been a long jumper in high school, winning Xinchun's track meet with a record-setting leap of four hundred and forty-five centimeters. Although the condition of his body was far from prime, all the extra fieldwork he had to do because of his absent brothers and old father kept him at least healthy. He flexed his biceps in front of Tao. "You think this body will get me in?" he asked, half jokingly and half self-consciously.

"Maybe," Tao said. "Would've been better if you'd have taken some of your dad's medicine."

Ming folded his arms. "That stuff is worthless."

"That stuff is your livelihood."

The two friends left Tao's yard and rode their bicycles between the apple trees of Tao's family's orchards. They made their way to the bank of the Yellow River, where they'd always gone before important moments to skip rocks and think. Ming had kissed Tao's sister here, underneath a willow, its branches dangling over the churning river. The two of them were barely seventeen. He had known then that she would not be with him for much longer. She was smarter than he was—top two percent—and she was the village beauty. For his entire childhood, Ming had thought the two of them would marry. Now he was trying to play catch-up, not even knowing what country she was in.

"If we both made it to the city," Tao said, "and had to pick one thing from the village to take with us, what would you take?" He took off his shoes, socks, and shirt. He stepped into the clay-colored water, cupping a handful and splashing it on his face.

"Nothing," Ming said, picking up a smooth, black stone. "I'd just take myself: my mind and body. I'm done with everything Xinchun." He arced his hand behind him, pulling the stone back as if his body was a slingshot, and then launched the stone into the river, where, bouncing once, it disappeared into a frothing wave.

Old Wisdom was worried. He was totaling up the day's profits and it occurred to him that he had sold the tiger bones too cheaply. With the cost of shipping and the labor involved in its separation, he should've charged at least five or six dollars more per gram. Ming was a smart kid. Why hadn't he caught it? Or, if he had, why hadn't he said anything? Always thinking about other places, dreaming about a life not meant for him, the boy was careless. And ungrateful, Old Wisdom thought. If it hadn't been for the store's income, he never would've had enough money to bribe the family-planning commissioner, and Ming would've never been born. Now, like all of his children, the boy planned to abandon him.

Old Wisdom knew the dangers of living outside Xinchun. In crowded cities, life mattered little, especially the life of a young man from the countryside. He had read about factory jobs where bosses worked their staff to the point of exhaustion. The employees lived in the company's houses and ate the company's food, and naturally the boss controlled when they slept and ate. He might even control the schedule of one's defecation.

Here, in Xinchun, Ming would inherit a store and become a respected member of the community, looked up to by everyone as the village herbalist. The boy didn't understand how good he had it, how hard his father had worked to give him this future.

Old Wisdom took off his glasses and pinched the bridge of his nose. Observing his reflection in his outhouse's mirror, he saw that his beard was growing too long. Strands curled below his neck and touched his collarbone. He would need to trim it soon, else he would look ragged, and nobody would come to his store and trust his prescriptions.

The two men from the city slept in their cars: Zhang Sha, Director of Search, in his Mercedes with the driver seat inclined, and Li Tan, Director of Transportation, in the bed of his truck over a sheepskin blanket. The next day, they waited by the school until classes ended. They bought lunch from a vendor cart, and nodded to all the students as they streamed out. Smiling, they stepped on the butts of their cigarettes before going inside.

"Greetings," Zhang Sha said. "You all should be proud for having been selected to attend this assembly."

Li, the larger and darker colored of the two men, looking like a Mongolian, stood behind him.

The young villagers sat on stools in a semicircle. Ming was glad Tao had also been picked. There were ten of them, and, with the exception of Ming, all were still in high school. The cafeteria was about twice the size of a normal classroom, where grades one through twelve all had lunch. Located in the basement, the room's narrow windows were close to the ceiling. Grease stained the walls.

"We have connections with a variety of companies," Zhang Sha continued. "Some of our people are at hospitals; others have attained jobs in offices, getting paid to sit in a cushiony chair and drink tea all day. It all depends on how smart and dedicated you are, because once you reach the city, we don't want you to have second thoughts. When you don't make money, we don't make money." Zhang paused, taking a sip of hot water from a rusty Thermos. "This is why we offer an extensive training period to assess your potential so that we can fit you with the proper job. Best of all, both you and your family will be paid during this period. We understand that you need money to live in the city, and that your family needs money to hire people to work in your place here in the village."

Ming couldn't believe his good fortune. Now his father couldn't possibly object.

"We only ask one thing," Zhang said, and Ming sank back in his seat, waiting for the catch. "We ask for your dedication. During this training period, which can last for a few months to a year, depending on the person, you will not be allowed to contact your family, your girlfriend, or anyone else who might cause distractions. Simply put, we want you to succeed, and if you back out in the middle of your training, not only will you not succeed, we will have lost money."

After Zhang finished his speech, there was a question-and-answer period. Little Slope, the son of an apricot and pear farmer on the east side of Xinchun, asked how much money would be given to his parents when he left. "Five hundred," answered Zhang. "All up front. That should be more than enough to cover a year's worth of labor." Parched Well, whose father farmed the lands west of Xinchun's main well, asked how soon they were leaving. "Tomorrow morning," Zhang said. "We have a strict schedule. Can't waste any time." Finally, Ming stood up and asked what would happen if, after the training period, they still couldn't find a job for him. "That has never happened," Zhang said, picking up his briefcase and taking out several sheets of paper. "Although if it did, we'd simply drive you back here. You can think of it as a yearlong paid vacation. It's all explained in the contract."

When there were no more questions, the young villagers lined up in front of the two men to read and sign the contracts. "Give a copy to your parents as well," Zhang said. "We can't take you unless they agree."

Ming and Tao were last in line. The two friends made bets on who would complete their training first. Then they decided that it'd be best if they finished at the same time, so that they'd be appointed to the same company.

"I hope the old man agrees," Ming said. "You're lucky to have a supportive family."

"Not supportive." Tao shook his head. "They don't care where I end up. I won't even tell them about the five hundred dollars."

"Wish I could do the same. I'm not so sure that money is enough to convince my old man," Ming said, even though he was fairly certain it would.

His father had married off his sister because the doctor from Shanghai had come from a wealthy family. In fact, the doctor had given his father enough money for him to renovate the store, to install new windows and a new countertop. Ming and his father barely saw his sister anymore, and his father didn't seem bothered at all. Sometimes Ming wondered if his father loved any of them, if he considered his sons, his daughter, and his wife—when she'd been alive—as nothing more than extra hands.

By the time Ming made it back to the store, the line had passed the bicycle racks and reached Lao Mei's DVD and VCD rental shop. Alligator tails were in high demand, known to prevent disease and bring good luck. A few customers, seeing Ming, shouted, "Get me a good deal!" Ming, not bothering to lock his bike, brushed past them and rushed into the store.

"Where were you?" Old Wisdom asked. His hands shook as he scooped the powdered alligator tail onto the scale.

"Let me get that for you." Ming lifted the wooden ledge and went around the counter. With the spoon in hand, he said, "I have something important to talk about."

"Later. Not when we're busy."

It was close to ten by the time the last customer was gone. Old Wisdom, exhausted, sat back on his stool and left the door open to let in the summer breeze. He smelled apple blossoms from the orchards, wildflowers along the dirt road, and budding sorghum from the fields. Running an herbal supply store had taught him that this combination of scents was good for his health, that whenever he felt close to nature, nature was rejuvenating him.

Ming took advantage of his father's good mood and set the five hundred dollars on the glass tabletop.

"What's this?" Old Wisdom asked.

"This is what I've been trying to tell you. I went to the assembly today. The man from yesterday gave us this money for me to go to the city."

Old Wisdom uncurled the bills, counted them, and then laid them back on the tabletop. "Your father may be a cheap man. But five hundred dollars isn't enough to buy one of his sons."

"Nobody's buying anyone. I've spoken to Twisted Weasel, the fourteen-year-old son of Mao Bing, and he said he'd gladly help you out in the fields and in the store for only two hundred dollars a year."

Old Wisdom shook his head. "Those men from the city are crooks. Once they have you, they'll squeeze all the sweat out of you. You don't know how hard city life is."

"They warned us that it's going to be difficult," Ming said. He got on his knees, took his father's hand, and kissed it. "Dad, all my brothers are gone. Tao's sister is gone. And soon, Tao will be gone. What will I have left in Xinchun?"

Making his children happy was never one of Old Wisdom's priorities, but gazing into his son's eyes, which had a film of tears, and feeling how tightly his son held his wrinkled hands, Old Wisdom understood that this was the only thing his son had ever truly wanted, and keeping him in Xinchun was an act too selfish even for an old man like himself.

That night, as Ming was busy packing his bags, Old Wisdom paced in their center yard, outside of his son's room. On occasion he peeked through the window and saw his son stuffing clothes into two emptied sorghum sacks. They didn't have the time or money to buy proper luggage, and Old Wisdom knew his son would be recognized as a bumpkin as soon as he stepped off the truck. Well, he thought, at least the boy would have a place to eat and sleep. Who knows? Maybe all the hard work would show him how good he had it in the village. With any luck, he'd be back home in no time.

II

As the truck ascended the Blood-cloud Mountains, curling along the highway guardrails, a fog settled and Xinchun Village started to disappear. Ming saw fields vanishing under the fog like dreams, like lands winking in and out of reality. That morning, for the first time in years, his father had woken up early. He had cooked for him, prepared him scallion cakes and bean curd in vinegar—dishes his mother used to make—and waited with the other families while the men from the city helped the boys and their luggage up to the truck bed. Only six of the ten boys showed up, and it surprised Ming that the men from the city didn't go to their houses to collect the five hundred dollars they had advanced them.

"Can I have a piece of that scallion cake?" Tao asked. "My family didn't prepare anything for me."

They were still twisting up the mountain, the road bumpy underneath, and Ming had trouble tearing off a piece. He handed Tao an unevenly torn wedge, then asked, "When was the last time you went to the city?"

"Last fall," Tao said, "to sell off our extra apple crop. We didn't make a lot of money though; everyone had a good harvest that year. So for an entire month we ate all our dishes with apples and still we had to throw away half a ton." Biting into the scallion cake, Tao brushed crumbs off his pants, which were still muddy from yesterday's swim. "I'm going to miss Xinchun," he said. "Even if we'll be gone just for a year, I don't know if we're doing the right thing. A lot of people left when we were kids, and watching them get on a bus or tractor with such a huge smile on their faces, I promised myself I'd never be one of them. You think the driver would let me off if I asked him to stop? I can give back the money and walk home."

"Don't be scared. Those people who left were smart. They knew the village had nothing to offer them. Plus, with me gone, what're you going to do in Xinchun? If you stay, at least we'll miss it together."

Tao nodded, but Ming could tell his friend was still unconvinced. "I don't know if I want to work in the city. Like my father used to tell me, it's better to be a big fish in a pond than a big fish in the ocean."

"That would be true," Ming said. "Except we were both little fish, and Xinchun's opportunities, like its wells, have all dried up."

"Would the two of you be quiet?" Little Slope said. He was lying on the truck's wheel-bed, his arm over his eyes to block out the sun, trying to fall asleep.

The mountain path was the only way out of Xinchun Village. It took two hours to travel through it. The poorly paved road merged onto a highway, and when the truck neared the outskirts of Yuncheng City, the sky turned gray and polluted. Smoke rose from the local coal refinery and blended with the clouds. Parched Well coughed, his lungs unaccustomed to the air. The truck reached their exit an hour later, where the ramp was completely backed up.

Little Slope awoke and looked around. "What's going on?"

"Traffic," Ming said.

Little Slope tapped on the truck's rear window. "Hey," he shouted, "you in there. How long is this going to take?"

The Mongolian glanced in his rearview mirror, then rolled down his window. "None of your business."

"If it's going to be long, would you mind if we stopped somewhere? I need to pee."

"Sit down," the Mongolian said. "Don't say another word."

Little Slope sat back down on the wheel-bed. Ming wondered if this attitude was a part of the training or if the Mongolian was just an angry man. Of course, Ming thought, he had been a villager just like them, and the company couldn't find him a job so they had him drive the truck.

"Don't worry about Little Slope," Ming shouted. "He'll understand his place soon enough."

"Who do I look like?" the Mongolian said. "Who do you think I am? Another word from any of you and I'll drive a knife through your face."

Night had fallen hours ago. By the time they reached their destination, Ming could no longer tell what time it was. They were on the other side of Yuncheng, beyond the downtown area with the tall buildings and fancy restaurants, where he had hoped their training facility would be located. Instead, he saw two identical single-floor houses placed side by side, behind which there was a warehouse with blackened windows running just below the roof. Beyond the warehouse two rows of tall trees concealed the three structures from the road, and Ming could see faint glimmers of streetlamps and headlights passing through the trees. In front of each building, two or three men stood smoking.

"Leave your things on the truck," Zhang Sha said.

Getting off the truck, the six boys were asked to hold a long, coarse rope. They hesitated, but Zhang assured them that it was a precautionary measure, so they wouldn't get lost when he took them to their rooms. He led at the front, pulling a handle at the end of the rope, while the Mongolian held a similar handle at the rear.

The house they entered was barely furnished. A grocery-store calendar with a girl in a bathing suit hung from a wall, and a single couch—its cushions missing—blocked off the entrance to the kitchen. On it, two men in their undershirts sat eating black bean noodles and watching a table tennis match on a handheld TV. The only person who stood up when the villagers entered was a middle-aged woman wearing an apron, her belly swollen.

"They're here!" Zhang said. He took out the package of tiger bones from his briefcase and handed it to the woman. "Got this from the village," he whispered. "Should be good for the baby."

The woman gave the villagers a dismissive glance before looking at the package. "You know I don't believe in this stuff. Why do you keep buying it?"

"Take it for me," Zhang said, and then kissed the woman on the forehead.

Together with the two men from the couch, Zhang and the Mongolian led the villagers through the kitchen and then down to the basement, where five pairs of bunk beds filled the space from one wall to the other. Two sleeping men occupied one pair, and a man sat on the bottom bunk of another. A single light bulb illuminated the room. There were two buckets in a corner, and Ming knew immediately, even from the top of the stairs, that they were filled with feces.

"Go down there and join the others," the Mongolian said, taking the rope.

"Please," Zhang added. "Classes will begin tomorrow."

The door slammed before the villagers could move. They made their way down tentatively, lowering their feet one step at a time, the light too dim to make out individual stairs.

Ming had expected the conditions to be bad, but he never dreamed that anyone from the city could live like this, worse than even the poorest person in Xinchun Village. He took the bed closest to the three people already in the room, and Tao climbed up to the top bunk.

"This is bad," Tao said.

Ming nodded. He stared at the man in front of him, an old villager, forty or fifty, bare-chested, wearing only a pair of tattered trousers, and the man stared back with a grin on his face. "How are the classes?" Ming asked.

"Classes?" The man laughed. "You still believe there are going to be classes?" The bed partially blocked the light, and only half of his face was illuminated. "This is a place to die." He paused. "That's right. You are all going to die."

The other villagers gathered around Ming and Tao's bunk. "What do you mean?" Parched Well asked.

"He's crazy," Little Slope said.

"Your friends seem peaceful enough." Ming pointed to the occupied bunk beds behind the man.

"Hey," Little Slope shouted, "you there sleeping. Wake up. Is your friend crazy?"

The man stopped grinning. He seemed to have regretted opening his mouth. "Leave them be. They're here by choice. Like me, they sold their organs."

Ming saw a cut on the right side of the man's body. As if sheared by scissors, it stretched from his ribcage to the bottom of his belly.

"That's right," the man said, following Ming's gaze. "They're taking out my other kidney in a week. The big man, the one who drives the truck, he tells me they're going to gouge out my eyes, too."

"This can't be true," Tao said.

"We're here to find jobs," said Ming. "This is a training facility."

The old man shook his head. "I'm sorry. I don't know what came over me. I shouldn't have laughed at your misfortune. I've been here too long."

"I have to get out of here," Little Slope said.

The others, stricken, backed away from the man. Parched Well tripped over a bucket of feces. Little Slope ran up the stairs, and the rest of the villagers followed. They crowded around the door. Ming and Tao moved up to the front. "Open up!" Tao shouted, pounding on the door. "We want out!" Ming felt his legs growing weak as he tried turning the knob. Then there was a shove from behind, and his cheek was pressed against the cold steel of the door.

They heard footsteps. "Stop it," someone on the other side said. But this only urged them on. They were making progress. The door began to bulge. Just when they felt they needed one more push, it opened. Ming saw three men standing in front of him—the Mongolian and the two men from the couch. They pushed the villagers back, attempting to re-close the door. Ming felt a kick to his stomach. Undaunted, he pushed past them and ran through the kitchen. He leapt over the couch, glancing back to see a man pursuing him. He opened the front door. Another man was there waiting, and before Ming could run out, the butt of a rifle came crashing into his face.

He heard it distinctly: music. Violins, French horns, and tympanis, building and cascading like clouds during a storm, the raindrops in the air refracting light into rainbows. He thought he was dreaming. The last time Ming heard this rendition of *The Butterfly Lovers*, he had been visiting his sister in Shanghai. He had hoped her husband, the doctor, would give him a job in his hospital.

"Do you have any experience?" the doctor asked, and Ming told him about helping his father at the store, weighing and mixing herbal medicine, memorizing his father's prescriptions. The doctor shook his head. "No, that won't do. I'm afraid you'll need some real medical training."

His sister smiled at him, and then hummed along with the melody. She wore nice clothes—a sunflower dress, jet-colored hair clips, and sequined shoes—and Ming thought she looked just as pretty as Tao's sister the day she had left Xinchun. No one would've guessed that her sister was from the countryside, that the two of them were related.

When Ming woke up, he was no longer in the basement. It took him a few seconds to realize that he was inside a cage. The cage, designed for some kind of dangerous animal, was inside a warehouse, and it extended halfway up to the ceiling, where round halogen lamps made everything in the room glow a sterile white. The music was coming from a stereo ten or fifteen meters away. Next to it, several doctors circled an operation table. They wore square hats and green scrubs. Their gloves were a splattered pink, almost floral. Their white mouthguards moved when they talked.

"This one is going to America," one of them said. "We expect extra compensation."

Another doctor lifted a brown organ in the shape of a bean seemingly out of the table, held it up to the light, and then placed it into a white Styrofoam box. "Refrigerator," he told the man next to him.

Sitting on a chair a few meters away from the table was the Mongolian, and when Ming noticed him, the big man smiled and walked over. "See anything you like?" he asked. "Only costs you a million or two dollars to buy a kidney, more for a liver or a pair of lungs."

A loud noise drew Ming's attention to the other side of the warehouse. Next to the driveway, where a truck was docked, a stone furnace churned. There was a belt feeding a body into the furnace. Ming couldn't be sure, but he thought the long neck belonged to Tao.

"Just like you," the Mongolian said, "he liked to make trouble."

Behind the furnace, hiding in half-darkness, a body hung from a hook. The boy had long legs. His head rested on his collarbone, and his big toe, almost touching the floor, was blistered from walking in fields.

Since Ming's absence, Old Wisdom's days had become long and difficult. Twisted Weasel was the laziest boy he'd ever seen, equally bad at tilling the fields as he was weighing and mixing medicine. Old Wisdom missed his son, who he hoped missed him too. Harvest time was coming up, and without Ming's help he was unsure if he'd get through the season. The profits from the store weren't enough. Soon he might have to sell it. What then could he pass down when his son returned? Ming would be penniless, one of those landless peasants in the village who begged for food.

No, it wasn't too late. He'd collect all the sorghum himself if he had to, if doing it meant his son would retain his position in Xinchun. What did his tired, shriveled body matter anyway when it came to his son's future?

With renewed vigor, he returned to the task at hand: filling out new orders of tiger bones. The task, like most tasks, had been Ming's responsibility, and Old Wisdom remembered his son's complaint the last time he had to do it. Ming had told him that they should stop supplying tiger bones, because tigers were becoming extinct. "Nonsense," Old Wisdom had explained. "Most of these tigers were bred in captivity, with the sole purpose of providing the world with their bones."

In any case, now wasn't the time to think about tigers. He had his own problems. On the paper, in the blank indicating weight, he wrote down twenty kilograms, which was double the amount of the last shipment. Putting the order in the mailbox, he hoped that it would arrive soon, and without any unforeseen delays.

GALAXIES BEYOND VIOLET

Melanie Rae Thon

1.
Yes, it's true, the bees are vanishing, not just dying, but disappearing, buzzing away from the hive at dawn and not returning.

Their bodies are perfect:

On the seventh day, God did not rest: God began to imagine the honeybee and the flower. Time blossomed into light, the infinite possibilities of perception. One hundred million years of thought, and even now the evolution of love continues.

Our strange sister!

Who but God can fathom: two compound eyes, each with sixty-nine hundred lenses, four filigree wings beating two hundred thirty times per second:

Behold the honeybee!

Thirteen millimeters long, ninety-nine milligrams:

I make myself in her image.

As she flies, foraging for nectar and pollen, the friction of wind through feathery hairs builds a static charge, her body electric. Above or below, the flower opens: infinite blue, worlds of yellow, a murmuration of white shimmering into thirteen thousand eight hundred lenses. She's blind to red, but sees a universe we can't know, galaxies beyond violet.

So lovingly she lands!

Pollen jumps into the hairs of her charged body. Hidden in the flower's folds, she plunges the tube of her proboscis deep, flicks her long tongue, sips love's holy nectar. She can drink herself drunk and buzz away dizzy. Each time she rises, her body glows, dusted with pollen. All day she moves, transferring life one flower to another, fertilizing ovaries that swell to ripened fruit and feed the world: five thousand blossoms in a day: a hundred and seventy-five thousand in her lifetime: forty days:

Until her wings wear thin, until her tattered body falls and fails.

She pollinates apples, pears, pecans, strawberries: avocados, almonds, squash, kiwis: oranges, peaches, soybeans, cherries: papaya, pepper, mango, coffee: blueberries, grapefruit, cantaloupe, broccoli: lemons, limes, clover, celery:

Behold the honeybee who makes your life possible.

She is the spark between: without her, they cease to be, and we soon shall follow.

Imagine pollinating your own blossoms, scrubbing anthers, gathering pollen, carrying your treasure home in tiny baskets, remembering to dry it for two days at precisely the right temperature, returning to your fields and orchards, lying on your belly in the dirt or climbing high to fertilize each flower. You carry a tiny duster made of bamboo and chicken feathers. Too much is too much. One light dip, one flick, one flutter: *may you dwell in the open heart*: clear your mind of all distraction.

Brother, as we lose our lives, we will love this world. Here is the path to peace, kneeling on the earth, bowing to the flower, surrendering our will blossom by blossom.

2.

My brother who does not believe in time remembers the future: *72 Migrants Slain*. One survives to tell the story. One walks thirteen miles, pressing his hand hard against the wound in his neck. One eighteen-year-old man, protector and guardian of eight siblings, a pregnant wife, a grandmother in Ecuador: one boy who traveled two months and paid a smuggler fifteen thousand dollars to guide him to America: one who hoped to earn enough to keep his people alive, to feed them: this one heard all the others die ninety miles from the border.

We refused to carry drugs, and so Los Zetas shot us.
(One boy falls beneath the body of another.)
We came from Honduras, Brazil, Guatemala, El Salvador.
(So easily the body opens!)
We died with our hands bound.
(So easily becomes blood and bowels, legs twitching.)
We died with dirty rags as blindfolds.

3.

Butterfly, bee, bat, saguaro: hummingbird, moth, ant, ocotillo: javelina, hawk, rattlesnake, vulture: scorpion, bear, bighorn, quail: dove, owl, woodpecker, thrasher: tortoise, gecko, warbler, raven: iguana, whiptail, perch, cicada: cardinal, pine, cypress, juniper: willow, poppy, grackle, iris: yarrow, primrose, tree frog, sunflower: catfish, columbine, salsify, verbena: flax, gentian, tanager, lupine:

On the seventh day, God in His rapture said:
I make you all as one in my image!

4.

Brother, all day you measured time by gallons of water. Your route took you deep into Cabeza Prieta, to three emergency drinking stations where brilliant blue polyethylene drums sat cradled in steel frames, waiting for you to flush and fill, to purify with drops of chlorine.

A blue flag on a 30-foot pole flapped in hot wind to mark each station.

Most of the drums are recycled syrup barrels, donated by *Coca-Cola* because nobody, legal or illegal: nobody: white, brown, kind, or stupid deserves to die of thirst trying to cross the Sonoran Desert.

You've found the bodies, the ones left behind, skin mummified to hard leather, eyes pecked out, flesh so parched and poisoned even the birds refuse to open them. They fell two miles or two hundred feet from water. You've held smooth bones: vertebrae of a snake, skull of a rabbit. You've touched the dead: brother, father, sister, child.

At the first station, you found two drums riddled with holes, shot and stabbed, spigots pulled out and stolen, the word *AGUA* slashed with red paint, replaced with other words that wound and kill you.

Three dead quail hung upside down, dangling from the steel frame, feet tied with fine wire. Who needs words to read this message? You untied the birds. Living, each weighed six ounces, and its wings spanned fourteen inches. Mostly, the quail preferred to walk or run. You don't know why, but you love to see them flee on foot, black plumes at the tops of their heads bobbing.

In early morning, as they drift down from trees where they've spent the night drowsing, their sad, whoopeling voices burble up and out of them like cool water.

Dead and dehydrated, the birds weighed less than breath, wind and sand, hot dust choking you.

You and three other volunteers replaced the drums, unspooled the long hose from the water tank in your truck, and set the gas pump humming.

Any night, the vandals might return to slash or shoot, stab or poison. *Blue is good.* Any day, vigilantes might wait here, disguised as immigrants, tie you to a tree while they blast holes through the tank on the truck, puncture your radiator, nail your tires. *Blue means water.*

Vengeance is slow. Thirst has no mercy. The water they spill could save four hundred.

Traitor: you aid and abet, you comfort the enemy.

Every Saturday for five years you've come to the desert to sustain the dark horde, the ones who risk their lives for the privilege of slaughtering cows or plucking chickens, the alien invaders, willing to work twelve-hour days splattered with blood, slicing their hands, losing their fingers, the dangerous swarm, surging across the border, hundreds and thousands, ready to die, but hoping to pick oranges, pecans, strawberries, avocados, grateful to prune trees or wash windows, singing as they get down on their knees to scrub floors, scour toilets, prepared to paint your house, relieved to mow the golf course.

They look just like you inside: ribs, spines, femurs, clavicles. Their bones are small, but arranged exactly the same way, in precisely the same numbers.

At each station, you found trash and treasure: cans with their tops punched open, a knife with a broken blade, a bible, a hymnal, a woman's shoe with a three-inch heel, razors, rosary beads, a bicycle with flat tires. You found a white dove, carved from two pieces of wood, one for the wings, one for the body, sweatshirts trampled in dust, prayer cards, a baby stroller.

All too heavy to take, all too much to carry.

You and your companions filled five black bags with garbage.

5.

Home, alone in your bed, the new day just beginning, you press your cell phone to your ear, *Noemí, Nazario, their baby Idalia, Oaxaqueños*, voice notes to yourself, *Zapotecs we met at the third station*.

You washed and bandaged Noemí's feet. *Bruised and blistered, too swollen to fit in her shoes.* Water hurt, bones broken. You pulled spines from their hands. Each wound flared, hot with infection. *We gave them antibiotic ointment, moleskin, lip balm.*

You tried to persuade Nazario to let you transport them to a hospital, but *no, por favor—no, gracias.*

We gave them applesauce, mandarin oranges, salted peanuts.

Idalia was still flushed and fat, thriving on her mother's milk, *but yesterday the milk stopped coming.*

We gave them formula and a bottle, diaper wipes and six diapers. You tried again. *Your wife can't walk. Please, for the baby.*

Very softly Nazario whispered, *Si, por Idalia.* He meant there was nothing for her on the other side. *Suerte o muerte,* luck or death. He meant they weren't going back there.

6.

Nazario has made a sling of his shirt to carry Idalia. His back burns, cracks and blisters. The distance between life and death is forty-two ounces, warm water slapping a plastic jug, its weight tugging his arm, temptation his heavy reminder.

He won't drink. Every ounce is for Idalia. He flicks drops on her hot skin to calm and cool her. When he squats to rest, he fills her bottle one swallow at a time. *Here is your mother.*

He speaks now only Zapoteco, the dialect of his village high in the Sierra de Madre de Oaxaca, the language of his wife, the songs of his mother. Why insist on Spanish here? Why teach Idalia broken English? His grandmother begged him not to go. *I am old and forgetting.* He whispers to Idalia in Macaria's tongue. *You will be our memory.*

Every few steps, he drops a tiny scrap of colored paper, trash he's found and resurrected: a prayer, a poem, a map, a story, a path that leads home to his wife Noemí.

She is far behind or far ahead of them. They left her in the scattered shade of a mesquite. No word, no kiss, no baby's cry could wake her.

Sleep, my love. Let sleep heal you.

Now, in late afternoon, a blacktail rattlesnake flows into the shade and coils beside her. He has no wish to harm or strike, no need to warn or rattle.

In his fifteen-year life he's struck twenty-one times: woodrat, flicker, cottontail, gecko. Together these strikes equal less than one minute, bright flares illuminating ecstasies of time. After he swallowed the bird, he lay still for nine days, digesting. He can survive a year without food, seasons without water. Each day opens into the bliss of heat and light, the poetry of pure sensation.

He knows the animal beside him by her taste in the air, a scent he catches with one flick of his forked tongue, one tender touch to holes on the roof of his mouth, openings to the organ inside where taste becomes human.

He hears her heart: a stuttering vibration amplified by earth, her body to his, muscle to vertebrae. The footfalls of mice, the skitterings of lizards, the rasp of wrens, the whoops of quail come as voices in his own skull: he has no ears, no holes outside his head to open.

The wild human pulse shimmers up his spine, jitters his jaw, sets the delicate bones of his inner ears quivering.

He sees inside her body, perceives her as warm waves wafting into pits on his face, opening ion channels, triggering nerves to the optic tectum where vision refines heat to form a shivery field of radiant colors, an infrared thermal image: gold and orange, rimmed with turquoise.

A flame inside a flame: if he wanted to kill, he sees where to strike her. The core blazes red. The human heart hammers.

Noemí, Noemí, Noemí.

The water is hot now. Nazario takes one long pull and then another. He can't stop himself. Water spills on his face, spatters to hot sand, vanishes as vapor. Idalia does not move.

Idalia does not whimper. He drops the empty jug. One less burden to carry. The last ounce fills his mouth. He can spit it in Idalia's mouth or close burned eyes and swallow.

Noemí. He would weep now if he could, but his tears are salt inside him. He kneels down to cradle the child, to taste her hot breath, no longer sweet, no longer milky. He spits the water between Idalia's cracked lips, feels the warm stream, luck or death, pass between them.

When he tries to stand, he discovers his hips and knees have locked; his cramped muscles will not lift him. Now he must crawl or die, fall down on Idalia or try to carry her. She swings heavy in the shadow of his body. There is no one else on earth to love. Thorns pierce his palms. Sand burns his fingers. Three feet or thirty. They might live another day. They might meet another creature.

Through closed eyelids, Noemí sees the shadows of birds descending, two then five then twenty, bodies dark and beautiful, rocking in air, not flapping, wings catching light, feathers sparking silver, the shadow of one wide enough to hold her whole body: *Noemí*.

The snake uncoils and flows into the desert. He ripples when he moves, sinuous spine composed of two hundred eighty-four vertebrae, a pair of ribs for each one, thousands of elegant muscles to move them. As an embryo, a snake inside a snake, his secret self formed tiny bones that might have become legs, but didn't. So much easier to flex, to flow, to move side to side, to slide on sand without them.

Noemí Amaya offers her body to birds: they have come to shield her from the sun: God has sent them to save her.

7.

Illegal Immigrant Deaths Spiral to New Highs in Arizona: so many dead the Pima County Medical Examiner uses a refrigerated truck to hold them: three or four to a slot: little tortoise, quick rabbit: they could be anyone: a bird or a bat, a javelina with wings:

There is so little left of them:

My brother walks bone to bone, body to body. *Desierto Peligroso*. June, July, August: the worst still to come: a day in December when he will find the fragile skeleton of a child nested in the ribcage of her father:

But now, today, Nazario Amaya hears the voices of birds, the skitterings of lizards:

Now:

Nazario hears breath, blood: his child's fluttering heart: the claret cup breaking open.

8.

The honeybee flies three miles and returns to the hive to dance for her sisters, body abuzz, wings humming: a spin, a turn, tones rising and falling: in this way, she tells them where and how far and which direction to go to find the sweet well of holy nectar. Charged body singing with sound, she is their memory of the future: her dance in the present, in the eternal *now* of her existence, unveils the past and foretells a journey.

If she's sick, afflicted with viruses and fungi, unable to digest pollen, if she's dazed, high on the toxins in pesticides, she won't return: she'll die alone to save the others.

I see my brother's pale body covered with bees. They're doing their dance for him, buzzing and turning. He's not afraid. He knows where they go when they disappear. He's learning their language.

Be quick, I say. *We won't live long without them.*

ENCOMIUM: SUN

Gabriel Gudding

Professor I first thought of your employment of water from the kayaks of Anchor Illinois engraver of lake tops far from my daughter's eyes Clio of small years who lives in a city

beyond Pennsylvania. In an old house. On Belmont. She lives near you, in Providence. By sea. Narragansett bay, she talks and talks

near the Grand Banks, Georges Banks, with her few fish, Newfoundland fishery, near the Cod, overfished, the squaretailed Cod, mighty, the Haddock she lives near, not the Redfish, near Block Island. Provincetown

near Cape Cod, the Haddock there, far away, she lives far away

1 What do you know about a little girl, transhistorical dandelion

2   World woodchuck. Woodchuck to the world, bladder of halos. Bubble of heat. Blubber of light. I arose my mother arose my daughter arose, the lily arose, the river arose, the tulip arose, old ankles arose, Warren Williams arose and there were theaters in the toys,—because of you, you hang, an indigenous dandelion of dust. Lucretius says that you are the size that you appear to be. Which still begs the question—of what size

3   you appear to be.

4   Do I perceive you as big
because I was told you were big? What
the hell

5   All vertebrate bodies fitted with vents, mantled in chancres, swathed with blisters, grommeted by sphincters

You tear

and fold the gingham of fogs You come
through the Canada of space You signal green
from the crush of destruction You blow a tangle
      of crumpled shade from a copse of oak
You anchor

such dejection to us
> thank you. That

those eating millet seed, Those eating potato chip, Those unscrewing hooves, Those discussing a goose, Those who know Jim Behrle, Those eating the leg muscles of rabbits, Those eating a firebug, Those in the house of sorrow, Those in the ringing valley, Those using a haircomb, Those who hit their dogs, Those farting in front of children, Those eating kale, Those smelling of lake water, Those who are cows, Those delighting in mildness, Those delighting in goodness, Those cutting the little creatures, Those liking the cheese, Those liking the corn, Those liking the other yellow foods, Those crushing a boy's kite, Those who walk on the air, Those who lost it, Those who are swine, Those who are horses, Those who puked on a plaque, Those who rode a host of creatures, Those who sleep with women at night, Those who lie with dwarves, Those who lust for horses, Those who collect excrement and sell it, Those who collect excrement, Those that are busiest at dawn, Those beset by pains, Those who camp with joy

cannot but be a companion of you. Oak trees can't
 decline you

That you are here, above the copulation, in this par-
 liament of Natashas, this rehearsal of knees

I climb your light. I like you I feel personal toward
 you. I revere yr clambering ass. Yr vast va-
 nilla climbing, yr fat prickles falling, yr
 raining of crumbling yellows, yr immense
 lightball cuticle, beach of light, seaball:

flaming rippling pudding

blonde sun, pulsing rice grain, fulgent rice boulder,
 basically spewing bright wedding rice into
 the boards of the world

we are down here under you, bunch of breathlings.
 A family of wet, made by you, hung here by
 you, made fuzzy by you—WE ARE REAL—
 there could be nothing

   6 sun, thank you for coffee
      sun, thank you for Clifton
      sun, thank you for Clio

sun, thanks for television   that you made the curious mosquito—you made the really loud
 siren—all this an Iliad—thanks

we did not watch a gopher
we did watch a gopher
we did not watch a gopher
we did watch a gopher

a gopher, what is it?!

not something that really listens to music!
not something that really wears clothes!
not someone who tends the grass altho she appreci-
    ates the tending of grass!
akin to a woodchuck, akin to a stoat, akin to a mink,
    akin to a squirrel

this is gopher!

sun thanks for gophers
thank you for visibility
with which I can also see squirrels

> 7 How did Justice come to be allied with an-
> ger, ill humor, and quarreling?

Thanks for the sea
    that big Russian melodrama, beaten vault of
    fishes, battered waterquilt of horse muscle

That you electrify the doily of the genome
    and filter life through the moms

Thanks that you spangled the distant black with
 eyes

Because I am a great bee and want to escape. I see
 now windy pines. I see now a complete bath.
 I keep flying. I am a bee. I am among your
 pigs. Now I pass a school, its bell chiming,
 the children issuing. Now there are gray
 things. It is a field, it is autumn. There is
 garbage. I am above a spider. I am above a
 young girl chalking on the sidewalk

Why did you, a clear jar of firejelly, lather the poles,
 carve the sparks, slather the backs of all
 these oaks. And salve the black with a bat-
 ter of light

    8 Is this the world where my body lives. This
 Illinois.

Everybody knows the sun spread the mucus
 through the legs' lips and mixed the piss of
 dads into pants and everything has a groin
 that fits them, but the apportioning of the
 motions of sex is spread across the fields in
 a grid, a movement of every groin occurs in
 an interdependent network of bone motion,
 actuarial, the pelvic, the chest motion, the
 motion of each pizzle, the motion of every
 hemipene is noted and timed, of chickens

is controlled, the motion of the buttocks of pigs is controlled, the suckling motions of calves, the access of the faces of calves to the milk of the udders of the mothers the cows, is managed, the access of lips of piglets to the teats of pigs, the access of snots of lambs to sheep tits, the suckling thereof, is placed on a confederated schedule, death is now an immense method for making crap, the heat of a border is predicated on a conspiracy of access to the sexuality of other beings, to the groaning of horses, the grinding of the motion of horses, is to turkeys, occurs in the presence of pigeons, occurs before the deer and the varieties of the dominated, none of this will collapse under the decency of space, no longer the solitary completely private experience of defecation preferable to many vertebrates, the pork bones are already in the earth, the roads are even again on their eyebrows, I am busy pointing with my telescope through the bodies of these animals, I can see out of their nostrils, I can see out of their holes, my eyesight splits on their brain and is shot like water out of their ears, I am exploring the cosmos by pointing my telescope out of their vents, cloaca, anuses, out of their billions of asses I shine like an argus, I blend myself into the hospital, I am finally a fantastic patient.

Harrowing and narrow through my calendar the varieties of babies step like ghouls from the broken walls of slaughterhouses and stumble backward into their mothers who rise from their scattered atoms at last dry and warm and in the woods safely. And I spend a nickel at my anus all afternoon watching the clocks dump their hands into the sea as teams of prisoners gather on the hilltops and somehow bundled up in coats with nods and computation fashion rockets out of hair and make dozens of arithmetical little moon launches, and I have seen at conferences some lippy and over-confident people and have heard again the variant of the lecture made that mentions all the daft shit that fed the fuck that drove the gears that pulled the ass that bumped the press that caused this shit. We have not spent our lives as pilots. We are as much passengers as the animals are. I know we move our bodies about, the ones we inhabit, as if they are improbable pits we drag through the earth, and that our dancing is as if two upright cannons did so. First came the long years, then came the little ones that went by in a blur of sisters and announcements—and I had been hit into not growing and yelled into staying small—but the steep hill is full of heavy shit like trees, and the wind carries sparks made from burl fires, and the small ergs of the sparks, like thermal crumbs, tumble in front of farms and the farmers stand there armored and cloaked in litter, shit, and biscuits or whatever, and I expressly tell them fuck you and your fucking fuck farm, but they've smeared their semen on sleds and tugged them over bridges and they have stretched and ironed and launched the labia of their mothers and animals as kites and they tell me their triumphant and inviting vulvas are even now at the edges of orbit, and they assure me their own scrotums are blimps traveling through the density of history and other deep governments, and all around a thick, encyclic heaviness, stuffed with the floating smell of grain and everyone's eyeballs are just dents in the light, and they tell me not even the photons, who will waft for a long time into the gases of the knee-shaped and cerebroid nebulae, give a shit.

Daily Piglet Observation. Healthy well-nourished piglets run around and play, especially when the sow rises to eat. After a successful nursing piglets will often settle down and sleep. Milk is frequently seen around their mouths. Well-nourished piglets have tight, shiny skin and a thrifty look, i.e., "bloom." Piglets that are not performing well, have loose skin, look depressed, and have a "hairy" appearance.[52]

> We congratulate a Vermilion, River. We kayak. We congratulate, a bridge, thanks, you carry, us, the bridge, for holding, I saw them the, mo.ving babies, we mean, it even today, the Mill St, bridge at Pontiac. Ill.inois. And, that guy, who honked, you, honked, your honk, reverberating on the dam wall, thank you, we're in y.our, mid.st. All, of the daughters, in the waters, all, of the brothers, with the, others: you, are con.gra.tulated: thanks.for h.old.ing love,s tho, you, do.n't, think of it, like that, maybe, my friends from youth I, congrat.ulate, you, for, propelling my selves, into this, "time place," I congratulate, the waters, of Evergreen, Lake, Co.mlara's Park for supporting, the gramanoid weights, of for.aging hundred, and then thousand, of our, medium geese, crissum, crown and occiput, who are, little little, flesh boats. We congratulate, the geese, thems.elves, for having, such little he.arty legs. You're all, scaly and nude, and knobby legged, you pinioned, you squamous senators. Yo.ga, because, yo.u are, in this w[hurl]ed, I congratulate, you, all your,

---

52   Reese et al., "Baby Pig Management: Birth to Weaning."

ENCOMIUM: SUN | 139

lo.vely te.[ache].rs. I congrat.u.ate ants, for being cut.e, I have never seen, an ugly ant, even up, close, in those photographs, by E. O., Wilson.

I congratulate Clio, d[a[we]][la]ughter of her fa(r)ther, a.nd, Ma.i(réad) Brine, you have done, so well, in yr 18, yrs, sis.ter, of Mar.ina, for you, as we.ll, as Ma.rina, a.re a, ch[isle]ld, of letters, of ladders, child of answers, of elbows, child of apples, of bellows, child of rivers, of otters, child of sunspecks, of waters: child of tendons, thin, springing, both the tendons, of her ankles, and the tendons, of the allosaur: I congratulate, Clio and the arrargement, of things, that made her. You, are a child, of that cloud and that cloud and that cloud. You, are a sister, of that chicken and that chicken, you are a sister, of a sister. You, are a child, of fat and wheat and wide fish. You are, in no way, related, to any dogs, altho you are, and you like that you are, and all cats too, at once. Child of purple, child of cool canal.

For Clio, and the distance to her, the ac.cident, of her, the int.ention of e.very mindhe.art that ma.kes, we ccngratulate J.ohn Mui.r, the pays d'en haut, mud as a colloidal fruit, the river as a lung barn, angry people, seven little bit, seven clam river, theoretical hull speed, that we clean the toilet, the mantle, the honey cell, the ladle, a columnar crown, the fouled animal, bird work and culvert fuss, bilge arts, bioaccumulate, echinodermata your sister. Do justice to possums and cows. The abjuration of leather. We hoist Clio. We hoist house and unhouse: your unreadable library. "All that is beloved must be changed, separated, severed." Whatever causes the metals to sparkle. It is remarkable there are stupid persons. Be sad as in a zoo. As in a leaving outward. Potamalalia, outmouth. The raccoons touch our gravel. Riparian accipiters. Franz Joseph rifle. Accepting misfortune cheerfully. We praise too readily. All of it. Peristalted

HER MAN

Amy Cicchino

She scowls at the figure outside. He casts the pole with long, quick snaps into the canal over and over again, raising squirming and flopping forms, their tails anxious, their eyes full of fear. After brief measurements, he tosses them back into the water. She whines with excitement. She envies the man outside, the breeze in his hair, the grass bowing to his feet with each gentle blow.

The room is dull, the air inside stagnant. She sees the neighbor cat, Jack, exploring the bushes below their red deck. Jack's black and white tail darts back and forth as his paws push an entrance into the tall leaves. His mouth is greedy; his teeth are far too fast to grab and tear into yellow flowers, discarding shards onto the tailored grass yard. After the attack, the marred tickseed flowers are limp. They have lost their will to perservere in the potted plant below the deck.

She is offended by the cat's openly aggressive act. While she might sometimes tear at things that do not belong to her, it is only because her back teeth feel so nice gnawing against her man's shoes. She does not mean to cause the destructive ends. The short black hairs on her back begin to rise. Her lip curls, and an ugly snarl steals her face. Her emotions commingle. She wants to yell at Jack to stay away from her deck and approach it only when she is outside to chase him away; they then can begin a game of losing and regaining land. She cries at the heavy glass door, a strange whimper that escapes her parted, naked teeth. Stamping her feet in frustration, she jumps again and again in front of the pane, hoping her man will take notice.

He does not pay attention. The man's face is angled towards the water, preoccupied with the turning and flicking of the reel. The tall rod bends with stress into a frown. The man seems conflicted as his body, too, leans back with all its might. His feet separate so he can plant his weight in battle. She forgets the pane, the cat, and her dissatisfaction to watch him in this struggle.

The fish does not surrender easily. But she does not think too much about the fish at the end of the man's pole. She does not believe the man will hurt it or any creature because he is her man, the man that feeds her and rubs her belly with his foot while he watches sports recaps.

The fish is raised slowly out of the water. The body weighs on the rod and the reel struggles to rotate, begging the line to give way; it does not. The man's body also struggles, creating a strange sound as the line swings left and right, cutting into the wind. She leans her head against the pane, ears perked, to focus on the fish oscillating back and forth at the end of the man's line. The man dips a large bucket into the canal, filling it with water. His rough grasp pulls the hook from the fish's mouth, and he holds the animal's body taut against a long chart. The scales shine a ruddy red in the sunlight as the wriggling form twists and turns its tail in the wind. She leans her front paws against the sliding door to give her height.

"Mangrove red snapper," the man says aloud, tracing his finger to a measured spot that does not reach the fish's tail.

He walks to the side of the house and leans his pole against the garage. Then reappears at the sliding door where she is waiting. So excited to see him, she forgets the fish in the bucket and jumps to lick his hands in greeting. He grabs her neck, putting her outside on a length of chain. She knows he does not want her to lick at him and follow him while he's busy gathering his tools inside, and she is happy to oblige. Once in the sunlight, her ears fly back, her eyes squint, and she faces the wind; she gets the best scent this way.

Jack is below the deck now, his eyes transfixed on the bucket, which makes a watery *thump, thump, thump* sound from inside. She eyes the cat in warning. "Stay away," her stares say, "We cannot play now; I do not want to play. I am outside and smelling the wind." She closes her eyes to better inhale and enjoy the overwhelming scent of brackish water.

Jack peers from the deck's red boards; his tail flicks back and forth. She has always been fascinated by his calmness, but now she hears him lick his lips.

She opens her eyes: "And stay away from my man's bucket."

Jack takes two steps forward, emerging from the deck. She steps forward towards him, but her excitement has tautened the length of chain and pulled the nylon necklace against her throat. She knows the cat has realized this limitation: with slyness to his step, he approaches the exterior edge of the bucket, beyond the chain's length. He hops to his hind legs, grasping the edge of the bucket with his claws, and paws inside.

She is shocked at Jack's brazenness and lets out a bark of possessive warning. She needs to let him know that this bucket and whatever it contains belongs to her man, and therefore is under her protection. Jack drops to the ground. His ears flatten; his gaze leaves the bucket to identify the danger.

Her anger is arrested by her man, who opens the sliding door and, with heavy steps, walks to the bucket. He does not bother the cat but reaches through the desperate *thump, thump, thump* and removes from the bucket the snapper fish. The man and his power awe the dog and the cat; she sees Jack fidget with nervous excitement. With a few, quick movements, her man draws his pocket knife, grabs the fin of the fish, and makes a slit through the neck and up the belly of the beast. The wriggling slowly stops. The gills halt mid expansion.

The scent of oil and flesh grows strong. A fervor rises within Jack, dilating his pupils, pushing his whiskers forward on end. She should be excited by the cat's movements, but all she can smell is death, and the lifeless form that casually falls to the ground frightens her. The dog takes her length of chain as far from the fish as she can, turning around to escape the stench.

The man tosses the extra parts towards Jack. He stalks the guts and tail, dipping his body low as if they were still intact, still making the same *thump, thump, thump* sound inside the bucket, but they are only the immobile remnants of what the fish had been. The man has saved the head for her. He calls her name, but she is trying not to hear and not to smell and not to miss the fish and not to judge the man.

HOW TO KILL BUTTERFLIES

Laura Madeline Wiseman

When is your first bug? Is it the dead, dried fly on the carpet you move across with your new skill of locomotion: crawling? Or maybe the black-bodied ants behind your grandmother's house, the ones you'd build castles and moats for, then teach to swim across the brown water? When do insects arrive in the world-scheme of you? Is a green furry caterpillar the first that allows insects to populate your understanding, that lets you see centipedes in the sidewalk moss, mosquitoes sucking the blood from your chubby thighs, a silverfish scuttling across the kitchen floor?

Or is it not an insect you see first, but the idea of insects that you are introduced to? You, the insect inside your mother, clinging to the stem of her. You, throbbing, twitching, doubling in size, like a spider egg suspended in the corner of an unused window. You undetected for weeks, months. Then the calls out for the specialists with their gadgets and chemicals, their advice, their insistence on marriage. And your mother, where is she in this? Prone on the bathroom floor, not gaining weight as women tend to do when so infected, but losing pound after pound. She quits smoking because it makes her puke. She can't have a single beer without it heaving her insides. At the beginning of your gestation she weighs 145 pounds, and by the time your sack ruptures and you slide into the doctor's catching hands, she weighs 125 pounds.

When is the first time for lice? How many times do you get to have lice thereafter? Once? Twice? More than twice? The first time is in Fairborn, from a discarded mattress your stepfather caught you jumping on by the dumpster with a group of friends. In first grade, you itch your blonde ponytails, draw out a bug from under your fingernail, then another. You tell the teacher, who calls the school nurse. The nurse traps two lice on cellophane tape, phones your mother, and bestows upon her the creatures from your scalp.

Your sisters, you, and your mother queue up for the shower for toxins to be squeezed on your hair. Rub in, water off, wait naked ten minutes. Rinse. Repeat again in ten days. Bed blankets inside garbage bags congregate outside the screen door until bugs die. Everything saturates in poison, the couch, the carpet, the mattress. Your long locks are combed by the tiny teeth, each swipe whisked clean on toilet paper to rid you of your live treasures. You study the adults' brown and sleek segmented tails, the young with clear guts churning your blood, the white nits as unobtrusive as dandruff. "Don't," your mother says, taking the tissue of carnage from your hand.

"Why don't they make a sound when they die?" you ask.

When your stepfather arrives home from work he, too, must shampoo, even "down there," your mother says. He curses up the stairs, into the bathroom, and after awhile your mother checks his salt and pepper hair with the comb. She's careful and meticulous behind the ears, at the hairline where the bugs elect to assemble.

"Frickin' kids," he says.

The second time for lice is in Bakersfield, in a school district that checks heads monthly as policy. Line up the elementary school kids. In gloves the school nurse commences; one line is for students who must go home and one line is for students who may return to class. You go home. And again. And again. And again. Students may not have nits in their hair, those dead eggs.

After the third time, your teacher urges you to French braid your hair on lice-check day. "Strawberry blonde hair like yours is a favorite place for lice to hide. They blend in," she says.

Your mother threatens to shave your head. In California you live for two years, for the third and fourth grade, but because of lice you miss school, more than thirty days in one semester.

The truant officer appears at your front door. "She needs to be in school," he tells your mother.

"I want her in school, but they keep sending her home because of one nit."

"Comb her hair in the sunshine. You'll see them better that way."

How many times do you get to have worms? It depends on what constitutes worms.

You are staying somewhere, homeless again, though your mother will never say the word: homeless. You all stay with your mother's newest bunch of friends who get high.

There's an apartment with corrugated porticos for cars, a girl your age you play with. She has a gray tabby kitten.

"It has flees."

"What's a flee?"

"They suck blood, even human," she says, lifting up the hem of her white- and blue-flowered sundress. Along the inside of her thighs, small red dots. "Flee bites," she says. "Larry, my mom's boyfriend, says they're hard to kill. As hard as killing roaches."

You nod in understanding. The kitten between you plays with a fountain drink straw from the convenience store. It rabbit-kicks the striped plastic tube, bounces, flips. "What's that," you ask, touching the round raised bumps of purple-red flesh.

"Ringworm. Larry says it's contagious, so watch out."

Is it that night then or a night weeks later when you get up to use the toilet? You wipe thoroughly, but have an itch, so wipe again. Then you do the thing women do, though you don't know it yet, the check, the quick glance at the tissue to note the color, the discharge, the mark of the body's revolution. But no, you're not looking for blood. What you see shocks you, tiny white wiggling worms. Dozens of them. You wipe again, hysterical. Flush.

You panic. Do you have ringworms? They didn't look like rings. How did they get in your butt? Should you tell your mother? Your sisters?

You are never treated. You never see them again, but you worry about worms for years. Every time your intestines writhe, you wonder if it isn't worms in there, twisting inside, teeming tighter, roiling along the interior of you.

When you do get ringworm, you are twelve. And it's not actually worms, but disease. Fungus. Red raised circles of skin your mother coats in orange clear cream.

"Quit hugging your friends," she says.

"I don't hug them."

"I see you. One thing after another you bring into this house."

When is the exact moment you learn to kill? How many times does it take for perfection? How many insects must you destroy before you know how? At what point do you choose death over affection?

When you are ten your stepfather yanks you from the second floor down to the first floor to stand in the corner where you remain in silence. Each time you inquire, another ten minutes are added. After one hour you want to ask, but don't. After a second hour you do ask. Your stepfather says, "I forgot you were there."

On the weekends when you go out to play, you do anything to keep from returning home. You learn to pee outdoors. You call home to say you will eat lunch with a friend, though, usually, there is no friend whose parents can afford to feed another mouth. So you kick gravel across the apartment asphalt, dig in the dumpster for toys, stretch out in the grass as clouds pass above and chiggers insert their piercing mouthparts into your ankles and thighs, inject a fluid to dissolve and then eat your skin.

Behind another block of apartments railroad ties embank the next encroaching lot. Here trees extend, roots naked, the dirt smooth in between. Here slugs and snails graffiti the expanded wood, soft green in places, spongy in others. Glittery trails create a network of lace. Here you learn to kill.

A friend brings out a salt shaker, shows you what happens to slugs when seasoned. Their slick bodies melt, their eyes at the ends of proboscis stalks swing.

"That's gross," you say. "You're dumb."

"Only a girl would think this is gross."

This same friend teaches you how to rip apart ants and rolly pollies and how to remove the glowing butts of lightening bugs and wear them as a night-time jewels. Together you cover yourselves in firefly riches, a war paint signifying a battle you think you've won. But what have you won?

When you are not killing, you're home: things happen that you do not understand, but which implant into your brain. A colony of memories grow. You return to them and they become more ordered as time unwinds forward and unravels back. Your mother, your sisters, and you hide in the bedroom, the door barricaded, but your stepfather heaves through. Your stepfather's often distant gaze, as if he concentrates on something very important, but very far away. Your stepfather reaching into a closet while you watch from the couch. He lifts his polo, slides a sealed plastic bag under his belt, drops the shirt over it. He presses his finger to his lips and makes you promise not to tell.

How many times will there be roaches? How many places will they find you? Or do you find them?

In Bakersfield you and your sisters sleep on a waterbed in a room just off the kitchen. There is no wall between the kitchen and this room, only a brown refrigerator and a stained, striped green sheet your mother has hung. All the outlets spark blue and are haloed in black scorch marks. It is no wonder then that after long nights of drinking a man will wander back into that room where the bodies of little girls sleep, ages eleven, nine, and three, two blonde, one brunette. Pubescent. At eleven you've begun to sprout those terrible hard bumps that will become breasts. Your littlest sister likes to bump into them or worse, hit them. When you punch her back, she runs, screeching, "Mom, she hit me."

A hand rubs your butt as you sleep on your belly, atop the warm ocean of the waterbed, where underneath thousands of baby roaches scatter and stream if you lift up the plastic bladder of mattress.

You take the hand and move it. You think it's your mother's. She touches your butt sometimes, a love pat. The hand returns. You move it again. It returns, this time sliding under your panties, to the sponge of your ass. You move it. It returns. Now you're awake and feel the hand; it's hairy, thick-skinned, callused. You turn over and see a man, one of your mother's boyfriend's friends. "Hi," he says, his eyes glassy, wet, red.

"Go to sleep," you say.

"Okay," he says, waits, stares unfocused.

"In the living room."

"Okay," he leaves the bed and returns to a dilapidated couch and a flickering TV.

What about the others instances of roaches? You remember hundreds of roaches. And didn't you read somewhere that for every roach you see, there are ten you don't see? Does that then make a million roaches that have been within inches of you?

Roaches in the store converted into an apartment your mother rents. Roach antennae sensing the surroundings from an open box of pancake mix high, high on a shelf. Roaches on the floor, skidding, sidling as your cat Marbles chases them, bats their hard brown carapaces across the floor into crevices, corners, and under your school clothes bagged in pillowcases. Roaches in the three-bedroom apartment your mother rents in Des Moines. Low-income. Section eight. The man upstairs punishes his wife on the weekends with broom handles and the cord of the telephone. When he becomes psychotic, your mother calls the police. Sometimes the cops come.

Roaches on the kitchen table having sex, dropping tic-tac-sized egg sacks that break open and pour out babies upon babies. Roach legs inside mixing bowls stored in the cupboards. Roaches inside your clarinet, crawling out as you practice. Roaches in your hair, climbing up as you sit and watch the nine-inch black-and-white TV. Perhaps they too want to watch *Young and the Restless*, *The Cosby Show*, *Alf*. Roaches in picture frames, speakers, desks, the radio. Roaches in the bathroom, chewing on panties, the dried white stuff that has began to leak out of you during the month. Roaches in the bathtub. Roaches in the kitchen sink. Roaches treading water as you do the mound of crusted dishes. Roaches on your bed.

Roaches inside your sister's guinea pig cage, eating Pepe's feces and feed pellets, sucking up Pepe's urine and spilled water. When Pepe dies, your mother says to your sister, "I'll bury him while you're at school today." But when your sister gets home, Pepe's body is on the top of the kitchen trash, roaches on his black and white fur.

HOW TO KILL BUTTERFLIES | 153

Is there a hierarchy of insects? Some not so bad as others? Good ones versus bad ones? Are there ones you are willing to save? Are there ones who will save you?

When you are twelve and your middle sister is ten, your sister befriends a classmate who will later become a cheerleader and give your sister up like a fanciful childhood fantasy. But for now, they catch butterflies, tigers and leopards of the sky.

They don't use nets to pluck the insects from their free float in the air. They don't use jars to swoop down on butterflies sampling dandelion and clover. Rather, your sister and her friend move with deliberate slowness. They select their prey and follow it blossom to bloom, inching closer each time it lands, tiring it, building its trust.

Once it lands that final time, the black straw tongue probing the depths of the white clover, its six legs holding to the petals, its orange and black wings shut, your sister crouches beside it, takes one hand and with the thumb and pointer finger picks the bug up and imprisons it in a discarded beer cooler. On her fingers a soft, multi-colored dust.

You tried this, spent an hour mimicking their dance, and did, you remind yourself, snatch two butterflies, a yellow cabbage and a small violet-blue. Though the second one hardly counts, as you'd given up and sat leaning against the school's brick façade to watch your sister and her friend gather on. And then, you looked beside you where the bug rested, no bigger than your thumbnail. You cupped your hand to capture it.

"I got another," you say, but they ignore you, so connected they are to the hunt, and you wonder if you are skilled enough for the kill, if you are a killer at all. Perhaps you are more insect than human, more infestation than arbiter of death: the colony of memories that have grown in you.

It must be a particular week of summer, a certain moment in the revolution of seasons because monarchs are in abundance. The instant your sister abducts one, locks it in the white box with the others, a new butterfly appears in its place. On a normal day, as your sister and her friend brown in the sun, as their hair goldens, they cull one or two dozen monarchs, swallowtails, cabbages, etc. On this afternoon, they take prisoner more than a hundred.

Sitting beside the box you can hear the insects, their wings and feet ushering a slight creak, and, when your sister strides over and opens the lid a fraction to insert a new butterfly in the cage, a scent erupts, not entirely unpleasant, but dark, damp, otherworldly, not how you thought creatures who drank the nectar of sunshine would smell.

For one night, your sister and her friend keep the box, until your mother learns of it. "Let the butterflies go," she orders, "or I'll put you in a box." And you wonder which of you is imprisoned inside the box and which of you has the power to open the lid.

Into the field you return with them. But when your sister opens the box, no orange and black cloud explodes from inside. A handful of butterflies feebly fly off. The others remain, two hundred wings together, clinging to styrofoam.

TRUTH BE TOLD

David Armstrong

Truth be told, before he met Jeanine, there were some nights Edward played early Rod Stewart songs and crooned them aloud to his bristlenose catfish, a bottom feeder content to live its life skimming the floor of its tank.

"You're in my heart," he sang quietly—sometimes so low the words barely left his lips. "You'll be my breath should I grow old."

He did it because there was no one else to sing to. He was a soft man, soft-spoken, a droner, a party fixture without bells or whistles. Around Christmas at Proctor & Gamble mixers, you'd find him slumped by the punch bowl with the blanched-looking interns and featureless copywriters.

He's forty this year, and he's catching Jeanine just in time. Forty-one, to Edward, seems outdated, wifeless and alone. But forty—there's still hope. He met her at a line-dancing night for singles at the honky-tonk bar off 32, the Steel Pony. That night he mustered some seriously mystical wooing voodoo. He charmed her, made her laugh, walked her to her car, and pecked her on the cheek. He was everything he'd not been his entire life.

Four dates in, he's enthralled. It's like walking on cotton candy. The AC is out in the diner, the doors open, but the jukebox works like gangbusters, a rickety and raucous reverberation in the speakers. Little Richard bangs out "Long Tall Sally" as Jeanine hums along, releasing the wooo-ooooo-oooos in tender whispers. Her hair is pulled up furiously into a rumpled bunch. She fans herself with a menu and sighs. She's thirty, pale-lipped, with slightly rounded cheeks.

"You should come with me," Edward says. "To North Carolina. I apologize for the short notice. But I've had it planned for months."

Truth be told, he's had it planned longer than that. For the past eight years he's taken the same vacation. Same beach house. Same week of August. All alone.

"I'm a bartender," she says. "I take off when I want. If they fire me, big whoop, there's plenty other places that want my combination of talents."

"What's your 'combination of talents'?" he says.

"I can mix a perfect rye Manhattan, and I have these." She cups her breasts and gives them a bounce.

Edward's stomach goes jello-ey, his head swims. He's imagining her naked, and he figures if they go away, the implicit understanding will be clear. But he's nervous. He doesn't have what you'd call a heap of experience. He's thinking about this, but now he's also thinking about her job.

"I thought you worked with animals," he says. "You said you worked with animals."

"I've done a little bit of everything," she says. She waves her hand in the air like she's cutting through cigarette smoke.

He wants to press further. They've kept it light, and he still knows relatively little. But the other part of him, the carnal and desperate part, the giddy, little id that's been tucked away in the beating, pink parts of his soul, is steering the car now. It's veering headlong around the curve of understanding—yes, she said; Y-E-S.

They'll leave in two days and, he thinks, they'll defile every room of the house.

Truth be told, she used to dream of being a veterinarian. She worked in a vet's office briefly, but she lacked the schooling, and most of her days were spent cleaning cages. She sometimes held dogs as they drifted off under the anesthesia, never to wake up again, while their owners cried or walked out without saying a word.

She does something strange on the way down. It's nine hours to Oak Island from his house in Ohio. They start early, and it's just past noon when they reach the midpoint. He taps the dash and says, "No turning back now. We're halfway there!"

She's asleep and doesn't respond. He nudges her. She turns and snarls. She bares her teeth, snaps them like a hyena. For a second he thinks she'll tear into his shoulder. Then she slams back against the door, inhaling sharply. Her head strikes the window.

"Are you okay?" he says.

Her eyes, wild and searching, close. They re-open with an exhausted sort of calm. Her shoulders, which were up around her ears, melt downward, leaving her neck looking long and sensuous. In the v-neck of her t-shirt, her cleavage is visible. Her chest is tan in a way that suggests to Edward topless sunbathing. He's overcome by this vision of her undressing on the roof of her building. His mouth goes instantly dry.

"Were you dreaming?"

She slides down into the seat. "Sure," she says. "I was a lion."

"You hungry?" he says.

"Nah. You're a big boy, and I'm a grown-up gal. We can make the trip without stopping for food. Don't you think?"

Truth be told, he has a ritual. He stops at the Cracker Barrel just outside Winston-Salem for lunch. He does this on the way down and the way back. Eight years he's maintained this routine. In fact, now he thinks about it, the drive and the dinner might be his favorite part, slicing down through the United States in a luxurious show of personal freedom. He watches a fair amount of the History Channel and, as a result, thinks about the hard fought liberties allowed him through the suffering and moral fortitude of American men and women, all so he can depress the accelerator, feel the fuel pumping through the engine, a stirring vibration underscoring the catchy rhythms of new songs on the radio.

But oh. His breath judders in his throat. Her hand is on her thigh, which is brown like her breasts. A new wave of longing overcomes him. This year's different. Routine is out the goddamn window. Stopping to eat is most definitely wasting time. This year, the getting there is one-hundred-percent the point.

A delicate, white star emerges from the grass.

Truth be told, if the beast had any knowledge of such things, it would call the star *painted trillium*. It would call the flower's arms *pedals*, its tuft of splayed knobs stamens. Had the beast self-awareness, she might call herself *deer*, might classify herself as a whitetail. She might note her own thin but powerful legs, and her tawny fur, which has gathered burs in the undergrowth. She might bend the trillium down with her forehoof to admire the slender stem bowing gracefully, the crimson-stained center (which, to her, appears only as a hazy gray), before eating it whole.

But had the deer such a consciousness, she would also register the sound of squirrel as precisely what it is, rather than perceiving the flicked twig under the squirrel's foot as a sign of danger. Had she these powers of observation, she would not bolt, not flee all fleet-footed up the timbered trail. She wouldn't charge headlong through brambled forest toward the black swath of asphalt smelling of burnt diesel, acrid oils, and exhaust.

The deer—had she known the flower, had she known the squirrel, had she known herself—might have named the boundary *road*, might have stolen road's power with her naming, like Adam from the Bible, might have fixed dominion over her own panic through the intellectual re-appropriation of objects, converting them into intellectual artifacts abstract enough to be prioritized, warranting gradations of alarm.

This the doe would have done. And stopped. Before bounding over the guardrail into traffic, stiffening in bloodless awe of the charging metal beast, which she would have dubbed *car*.

There's too much blood for perspective. The shattered glass. The dented curve of the hood, the roiling fresh smell of burning grass—or is it an earthy aroma, twigs and fecal matter, nuts and bone?

Edward makes sense of only a single hoof, which has reached in through the safety glass like a jagged pike. The animal's neck is broken across the frame which separates the passenger-side window and the windshield. An artery has been severed. Blood flows out in softening gushes down the vents, the radio, Jeanine's legs.

He reaches for Jeanine's knee before looking at her face. She's been thrown forward into the hoof. There's a gash in her neck, flowing, and she's slowly, almost absentmindedly, dabbing it with her fingers as if she's feeling for a blemish. A cut over her forehead turns her tilted ear into a small bowl for blood.

His head aching furiously, Edward scrambles from the car and heaves the hot deer from the hood. The body is heavy and comes away with a tearing sound, slumping slowly against the fender.

Edward slides back into the driver's seat, finds a chamois in the footwell. He presses it against the wound in Jeanine's neck.

"Can you hold it there?" He keeps searching, but sees no cars.

She nods weakly.

"Keep it pressed tight," he says.

The center of the rag blurs into a raspberry-colored blotch.

"Stick with me," he says.

And were Edward given the gift of elevated awareness, like that granted a deer which knows her own name, he might, in that moment, discern a ticklish double entendre: stick with me. The tacky blood sticking her clothes to her skin, but more importantly the long-range implications: stick with me—stay with me forever, be my wife, my lover, give me children, press your elderly and enfeebled hands in mine on our fortieth wedding anniversary and thank the good Lord as our children and grandchildren cheer our life together.

Stick with me.

Truth be told, he's waited so long for someone to come along, he can't fathom it not happening. When he was a young man, he used to wonder what was wrong. Why hadn't he met someone? He spoke slowly, yes, and women seemed to find him funny in an unflattering way. He kept a dog for a little while, and the dog was loyal. The dog's name was Cody. But Cody barked and barked all day long, when Edward was at work, and the neighbors complained, and he gave Cody to his nephew, who swore he knew how to "dog whisper." A year later, Cody had disappeared. When Edward came to visit, he was too polite to ask what had happened.

At this speed, the car bucks and wobbles, cresting hill after hill. No exit. No town. No hospital. But a fog has begun churning in Edward's mind. Why would he need a hospital? He's forgetting. There's a knot over his right eye that's begun to swell; his head must have struck the steering wheel. He touches it lightly and slows. No hurry, no worry, he thinks. He tries to reassemble the scrambled pieces of his brain. He gets the sense he's forgotten something. A white web of pirouetting sunlight appears in the fissured glass.

"You'll be my breath should I grow old," he sings softly.

He's thinking of their life together, he and Jeanine, as she sleeps beside him on their first vacation.

Truth be told, she found out she was pretty a long time ago. When she was fifteen, men stopped being able to hear her. It was as if she were speaking in a dog-whistle voice. Average ears didn't register her questions about biology, about menu items, about lumber for her patio or the life-expectancy of tires.

"This is a man's world," James Brown sang on the radio. And Jeanine sang along to that with a hallelujiah-hand held high over the steering wheel as she drove. She thought about buying a dog, someone who'd listen, but still couldn't bring herself to take on that responsibility.

The house overlooks the beach and sits on beams that raise it above high water. Edward pulls into the carport below.

"I'll take our things up," he says. His speech is slurry and garbled. "Why don't you go down to the shore." He opens the trunk and hauls out the luggage. He totes it all up to the bedroom and descends again to find Jeanine still sitting in the car. The bloody rag is stuck to her neck. She's staring blankly out the obliterated window with eyes filmed over.

"I thought you were going to the beach," he says.

He's still having trouble with his mind. The gnarl of sexual anticipation inside his stomach has petrified. He lowers his head to hers. Her breathing has the same rhythm as the waves breaking along the shore.

There's still time, he thinks. For incomparable sex and a life together. He refuses to hear otherwise.

"Still time to get to know you," he says.

Truth be told, when she was only five, a neighbor boy, home from college, babysat her and her sister. Her sister was three. He drove them to the beach—they lived in St. Augustine then—and the world was hot, the aching summer practically blistering the leather seats in the car so that she and her sister were forced to tuck their dresses beneath their legs.

The boy told them they were on an adventure. They parked at the seaside and he cracked the windows. Then he left them there. Jeanine could see him beyond the hood of the car meeting his summer fling, a long-legged girl with dark brown hair down to her denim shorts. The two of them pawed at one another in the shadow of a deserted pier while Jeanine and her sister surveyed the sand and the ocean and the rising surf washing its white into the beach. It got very, very hot. Her sister stuck out her tongue to express how dry it was. Jeanine took her hand and told her all they had to do was to wait and not get in trouble.

Another car pulled alongside them. Jeanine and her sister hid. After the people got out, she rose up and looked into the other car to see a small terrier staring back at her.

The terrier began to bark. Jeanine barked back. She made a game of it, testing the cadences, the ferocity, the pitch, to determine the dog's language. The dog heard her and seemed to understand. They barked at one another for a very long time until the college boy came back.

By then her sister was dead of heat stroke.

That's what this feeling is like. The heat making her brain a woozy mess. The man is speaking to her, but he's lost sight of reality. He's slipped. He's apparently, reverted to his own desire. He's whispering about her joining him in the ocean, about finally, the two of them consummating—he's using that word. He's talking about grandchildren. The air has cooled, and her eyes have gone dry from being open too long. Blood has congealed down her shirt.

She remembers only the impact. But now—well—

Sweet Jesus, I need to make this happen myself, she thinks. I need to make my voice goddamn-well heard for the first time in my life.

Or something like it. Her thoughts have lost the shapeliness of words. She's become an entity of instinct. She has an unabating desire for survival. On some level, she knows the man has turned her into something carelessly remade out of his own need, like many men before. She's never felt this weak.

The sun drops behind them as he carries her to the ocean. A chill comes over her as the saltwater soaks her shorts, her shirt, caresses her stomach in a fine wash of foam. The water fills her mouth. She heaves a tiny sputter to keep from drowning in it.

He kisses her cheek. A part of her doesn't blame him. He strikes her as needy—in need. Maybe he thinks he can love her, and she him. But love, as a large thing with a span of decades, is too elusive. Love to her now, truth be told, would be a simple moment of rescue, a rush of relief from the oppressive heat.

He's whispering to her now. He seems to recognize the fact that he's committed an error. He's scared and loosening his grip.

"I'm sorry," he says. "I'm sorry."

She feels him letting go.

If the ocean were aware of the people near it, it might occasionally manifest a helping wave. It might gently spritz the young lovers on the beach in a cold shower that sends them trundling back to the car, their senses regained, to save two neglected children from the heat.

The ocean might recognize one man, dazed and acting out of his own shock, carrying a near-dead woman into its watery embrace. The ocean would glean this man's desperation, his need for love, his act a hopelessly and idiotically romantic gesture garnered from his muddled ideas about love's cruelty. The ocean would slap him with a flat, cold swell. It would show him the woman's shallow breathing, her unvanquished life clinging to the night air. It would save her.

It would save him.

But, truth be told, the ocean is not aware, the college boy was not aware, the deer was not aware, and Edward, in his holy thrall of the what-could-be, has never been aware, has in fact been so blind with desire as to never see Jeanine at all.

You can't count on any of them, she thinks. And before the last wave can shove its way into her nostrils, she summons her hand to rise from the water, to clutch the man's hair and bend him to her.

He looks stunned, she thinks, to be pulled this way, and he responds slowly by puckering his lips toward hers. But she yanks his head to the side so she's speaking into his ear. She forces the words from her mouth.

"See me," she says. It's the unpardonable language of hope, a command that might have saved her sister, the deer, and the dog.

"See me," she says.

See me. See me. See me.

THE END OF THE LINE

Olga Kotnowska

Señor Alejandro moves in between days. It is how he lives: he lives in between days, he strides along corridors, corridors of his mind and of his forests, of his pastures and of pastures that are not his, and time is something else to him.

And when asked, his neighbours cannot say where Señor Alejandro ventures between dawn and dusk; sometimes he ventures between dusk and dawn, and his neighbours do not know where he goes.

On some evenings, Señor Alejandro does not venture, but sits on his porch. Through the tangle of green that grows along the wire of his fence, he can be seen. When he talks to passersby that stop by his fence, he talks slowly, and his words are accompanied by a look that does not remain on the surface, but digs. Sometimes he offers his horse—but never his best horse, the chestnut mare that shines—for the walk to Las Montañas. The walk from El Valle is long, across three rivers that have grown with the recent downpours.

Thunder rattles today, from beyond the valley it rattles, from along the ridge of the mountains that cover the Caribbean Sea. Señor Alejandro rides his best horse, the chestnut mare that shines, along the secret road to the cascade. He taps the sides of his mare with his boots and clicks his tongue, and she quickens her pace. He clicks his tongue and she knows, her long snout bounces to the rhythm of her trot.

From the peak of the valley along the road, muddy after so much rainfall, Señor Alejandro sees the grand tree. It emerges, rises high from the surrounding canopy, dark like charcoal, darker against the canopies that are green. At their tips the branches split, their fingers splay out, reach further towards the empty space where the crowns of the tallest trees do not reach. The trunk is broad even at the shoulders, and this strikes Señor Alejandro; he thinks of the trunk, imagines it running thick into the ground, thicker than promises and women's braids. His grandfather once told him, *This espavé, it is my friend*, and his grandfather paused because this is what he did before announcing something of weight, and when he continued, the hardened lines of his lips almost showed a hint of amusement. *You can talk to it like I do, but be careful, this espavé knows more than me, and it knows more than my grandfather and our fathers before that.*

Señor Alejandro looks at his hands—they choke the reins. He looks at his hands, his hands and his fingers, short and thick, the curves of their tips rimmed by hard edges, dirt ingrained in the lines of his fingerprints. And now when he stretches his hand, when each finger reaches away, creases crash against one another: the waves of an angry sea. His hands, his very own, are layered by wrinkles, and they are a reminder of time because he has no mirror, he does not see his face in a mirror.

Today, he is the grandfather, and this tree—this grand tree that he has passed many times—knows more than he does. If he were to stand beside this tree, Señor Alejandro would be young still, and when he thinks this, he chuckles and his body bounces against the saddle, and when his cough rips through it, his laugh ends.

Together with his mare, Señor Alejandro follows the track, the only track that leads to the secret cascade, and to their left the valley opens up. From the peak of the mountains, the valley all the way down is lined with treetops that are green, and the sky is marbled with greys and blacks and whites. And today, after a whole night and morning of rain, the sky has grown quiet but the world is heavy, so heavy today with the mist that hangs and spreads, tumbling down the mountains, down along the green lining of the valley, swallowing it all. And then this tree—this grand tree on the other side of the valley—it pulls at Señor Alejandro, and so he turns his back, glances behind him, but the mare continues forward. She knows the path to the secret cascade, and so she pushes forward against the green that begins to grow darker, more fierce.

Señor Alejandro whispers with his calmest of voices, *Easy darling, easy*, and this voice he reserves for his mare only. He clicks his tongue, runs the flat of his palm up and down her neck, presses against the silk of her skin, presses so she feels it, and so he feels it, too, through the calluses and through the rough layers. The mare snorts, her ears flicker, and Señor Alejandro looks back.

He looks the espavé straight in the heart and he knows one thing: he knows that he has outlived this master. Soon this tree will fall because it stands but it does not live. From afar, from where he and his mare ramble, the grand tree bursts with patches of green, but Señor Alejandro has been around long enough to know that its branches are bare. The green that lives in the pits of its bark, across the body of its trunk, around the limbs of its branches, and off its branches into the canopies of the forest: this green does not belong to the grand tree because it is given by the lives of other plants. Underneath all the mosses and orchids and creepers, the grand tree's bones are brittle, any day now these bones will come undone. The tree is not as it seems: the tree is like life. If he had the chance to tell someone, Señor Alejandro would say, *Life is not as it seems.*

And he thinks this and he winks at his mare. He is about to say something that weighs the mass of his world, and so he winks not once but twice, but the mare knows already because she had witnessed it all, she had seen him after the hurricane entered his heart and left it flushed out. Señor Alejandro does not need to tell her, but he tells her again. He says to his mare, *Darling, life is not as it seems.*

She was never going to be there for the long haul, his wife. Señor Alejandro never found the opportunity to tell her that he is not made of crocodile skin, that his is not like the skins of all the other men. All the other men, they come from some other place, they belong to something else. She broke into his heart during the days when he thought he did not care for love, and so she took him when he was vulnerable, and when she took him she took him whole, she took the whole of him. It was never going to end any other way, because when a woman offers you her world, how can you not fill your lungs with it all, how can you not fill your lungs with everything on offer and then demand more?

And now Señor Alejandro can see it: this is where he went wrong. Everything she did, she did with unsettled eyes. Always the green of her unsettled eyes. It all happened by accident. She came along during the days when he thought he did not care for love, and so he was unprepared, untrained in the art of unlatching a heart.

When she took him, she took him whole: pressed her skin into his, folded her body to fit into his gaps, slid her forehead into the warm pit of his arm, and fell asleep with whispers and with grips. Like this, she took him straight into her world until the day when she pressed her lips hard into his ear, loveless, used up. She said, *Remember this like you remember your mother's name: things change, things don't stay the same.*

The rain falls under the upturned brim of his straw hat, tattered down to only its strongest small bones. Señor Alejandro curses. The wind is not strong, but the thunder continues to roll from over the ridge of the mountains, and the mist spreads out even thicker, closes in on the valley. Where mountain faces stood high, there is now nothing, there is only white—and is this what is coming for him? He curses again.

Against his thick shoulders and down the slight bend of his back the rain is heavy. At this time of the year, the sky lets it all go, abandons the rain to fall over fields and forests and rivers. And so the rain pushes against his hat and Señor Alejandro folds the front of his brim back down, squints his eyes, and, together with his mare, makes the descent down the track.

He had sculpted out this track, it seems, in another time, before the back of his hand was an angry sea, and before he ever thought of all this, of the penalties of unmeasured time. He pushes on, but the mare is slow. Down the steep track of rocks and mud the mare places each foot with care, and sometimes under her hooves the mud slips, but Señor Alejandro holds on. He trusts her, and he clicks his tongue and presses the palm of his left hand hard across the side of her neck so she feels it, so she knows. And he does not need to lead her because almost every day they come through here, and she knows more than he now. He gives it all to her, he lets her choose the shortcuts. She knows more than he where they must turn to avoid the knots of growth that, with the season's rainfalls, have invaded untouched frontiers, or the newly fallen trunks that have cut their track.

From underneath his hat Señor Alejandro whispers, *Easy darling, easy*, and he does not do this because he needs to. He talks to his mare because this is how they are, this is their life: she listens and he talks and he almost never needed anyone else.

The waterhole sits in the pit of a cascade wall that stretches up high, almost vertically. Señor Alejandro was never able to judge where it ends because the wall soon disappears under branches and leaves and vines and roots. It does not rain down here, so Señor Alejandro folds the front of his brim back up, wipes his eyebrows with his wrists, his forehead. Down here, this place is almost untouched by the caprices that reign out there, beyond the green ferocity that presses against the waterhole from above and from everywhere else. Underneath the thick roof of the foliage, the waterhole is governed by the clicks of its own metabolism: it is slow, sometimes it is slower, and sometimes, when Señor Alejandro wants it, everything becomes still. This is his heaven, here.

Señor Alejandro dismounts the mare and his body stalls, slow to respond to these movements that he should have given up a while ago now. He gathers himself together, forces these bones that are almost eggshells. He works the saddle off, and it is the finest thing he had ever bought, with a seat of red velvet: and it was the only saddle fit for his mare. He undoes the straps without thought and pushes the saddle off, lets it fall to the ground. He presses his nose against the wall of the mare's snout, he breathes in the smell of home, the dust and the skin and the dirt. He presses face against face and his mare does not back away but stands still. He reaches underneath her head, strokes along the trench of her jaw, smiles when she snorts and then tickles the sides of her neck. When Señor Alejandro pushes his look into the black almonds of the mare's eyes, this he does softly, and he sees his mare look straight back at him, her eyes growing softer when he whispers to her. Or this is what he believes. With his thumb he presses the white diamond between the mare's eyes, imagines that he stamps the pattern of his fingerprint. This is his gift to her; this is for her to keep. This is his mark.

He stamps his fingerprint into the white diamond between the mare's eyes, and this is how he marked his wife the few times he had almost had her back again, or this is what he had thought. After he made love to her and she grew docile, submitted, and while she slept, he heard her unsaying all the lethal words with which she had slowly began to drown him. In those moments she was his but not quite, and so he would stamp his fingerprint between her heavy eyes. He knew it all, he knew that his wife was never going to be there for the long haul, he knew all this because he is not a stupid man, but a man who had never learnt how to unlatch his heart.

Señor Alejandro pulls away, steps back. He wonders, will everything pause? He contemplates the waterhole because he is ready, almost. He looks at his mare and he thinks of loss, and this he knows well: loss. For his mare he has no words because what could you possibly say? He whispers, barely whispers, *Darling, you go*.

He wants her to escape from this place, he wants her to run past El Valle and past all the other villages, away from the men that will chase her. Of this Señor Alejandro is sure because he has been around long enough: all the men will chase the chestnut mare that shines. And sooner or later, they will drag her down along with their own insecurities. He wants her to disappear because when he thinks of his mare belonging to another man he begins to feel faint, and he does not have the strength to think of this. He points with the whole of his hand but in no particular direction, whispers, *Darling, you go*.

He turns his back to her and he breathes slowly because this is all he can do, he can only breathe slowly now as he nears the waterhole, as he tries to tune himself to the rhythm that pushes life along down here. With the whole of his body and with the whole of his heart, and against the strongest of wills, he wrenches himself away.

In the waterhole, Señor Alejandro falls back and lets the water catch him; he lets go and looks up and feels alive. The water is smooth along the tired creases of his body, softening him up, softening the layers of skin that had been growing over wounds never repaired. He presses his back against the smooth rock wall of the cascade, and as the stream from above sluices across his body, hits hardest against his shoulders, he feels touch, and he feels alive. He weeps. He weeps for this and that, but mainly for the knots that had been placed across the whole of his life, knots tighter than clenched fists: placed by women, by a woman. And the only thing women have taught him is loss.

He reaches for the bar of soap that he hides in a crack of the cascade wall, behind the waterfall, and he washes his chest in circles, washes along the ledges of his collarbone, and when the white square slips out of his grasp and drops into the waterhole, he does not have the bones to chase it. He thinks about the beginning of the grand tree, because he thinks about beginnings often now. He thinks, when you come to endings, you go back to beginnings. He thinks, before that espavé was grand, it was only a seed. And his eyes are closed but he can see, and he sees this seed under the sea of dead leaves, in the place where the grand tree now stands. And he sees this seedling small and frail and lost and almost impossible, barely off the ground, waiting under the shade of its grandfathers, waiting for one of them to fall and let the light in.

And when Señor Alejandro thinks of endings, he thinks of his grandfather, and of the grandfathers before. And he thinks of the grand tree, anchored by the highways of its roots; and the highways don't run deep but they run far, they run far across the earth. And now this tree knows the earth so well, and with the traffic of ants across the craters of its bark, and with the vibrations of the woodpeckers' taps that search for food in the tunnels under the tree's skin, and with the borrowed green that colours its dead limbs, this tree is a city, and it knows life so well. And this tree is not the end of the line because over its past it had spread its seeds, out across the valley it had spread its seeds, and maybe even over the ridge of the mountains, and now this tree will fall but it is not the end of the line.

Now he himself will fall, after eighty years or so, but he is the end of the line and his mind ticks and there are many thoughts now, because when you come to endings you go back to beginning. He asks, does he know life so well? and is he a city, and is he knowledge and history? And he too knows this life, maybe a little too well; he knows the smell of the seasons and the smell of storms, and the smell of change and of deceit. And he knows of the cycles and of the comings of things, but he is not settled because he thinks: I am the end of the line, and he does not have the patience or maybe the courage to think of his place in all this.

He dares a look across to the bank, sees the mare looking at him, standing still. Even from afar sees he sees her eyes soften up and it is all for him. From afar he sees it all again, looking at the cut of his mare: a body made of sharp curves, beauty down to the body's finest bones. He waves his hand in no particular direction, but the mare does not seem to understand this command of his. Or maybe she chooses not to, maybe she is ignoring his words by choice. And so maybe she is not his after all, maybe she never was. Maybe nothing ever was.

It is too late to panic, pointless now, but through his corroded lungs Señor Alejandro begins to breathe faster. He gasps. He is leaving nothing behind but a stamp in the white diamond between the mare's eyes, and is the mare even his? Has he been tricked twice? He feels shame, or something akin to an impulse of having to fold yourself inwards to the smallest self you can be. He can do nothing now but imagine himself weighted with loss because loss is the heaviest thing he knows. He imagines himself sinking, and he is even heavier because he is sinking with this shame. And like this he lets himself sink, he takes his shame down with him; he takes his shame down with him like the strange men who had drowned with his wife, like strange men who will drown with the chestnut mare that maybe never even was his.

THE SKY ABOVE CHAIRS

Gary Barwin

The chair nuzzles against trees. It remains still, invisible to its predators. Looking is a contract between hunter and hunted. Also, hiding. Look at a chair. It looks back, waiting for what's next. The desk chair. The chair of another. The chair at rest.

A forest of chairs, a silent choir, the inverse of trees yet becoming trees. Moist pools of thought or sense. Inside the chair, a red city, a briefcase, an underground of blood.

Once, a house where chairs were everything. In bed. The garage, the rec room. Small childhood chairs. In the attic. In the breakfast nook. Old man chair. New baby chair. The carpets were chairs. We ate chair. Remember when we were young? When did they come to our home, the forest the size of humans, not chairs?

Once, in early spring, the chairs were in our yard. We spoke in whispers, as if before a house of cards. The chairs seemed telepathic, each thought shared between the group of chairs. They waited as one, then leapt the fence in a single thought, a flock of birds, their wings silent and invisible.

In the ravine, leaves unfurl, branches complete their plans. Clouds hunt the moon as the moon hides then disappears. We know the chairs are moving, but see only dust motes illuminated in a beaming slash of forest light, the scuttle of leaves on the forest floor, a scurry like the word *chair* whispered from nearby. Chairs, we say. Goodbye.

ABOUT THE CONTRIBUTORS

David Armstrong is the author of two story collections, *Going Anywhere* and *Reiterations* (winner of the New American Fiction Prize). Individually, his stories have appeared in such places as *Narrative*, *Mississippi Review*, *The Magazine of Fantasy & Science Fiction*, and *Iron Horse Literary Review*, and won *Yemassee*'s William Richey Short Fiction Contest, the *New South* Writing Contest, *Jabberwock Review*'s Prize for Fiction, and the *Mississippi Review Prize*, among others. Armstrong received his Phd in creative writing from UNLV, where he was a Black Mountain Institute Fellow and fiction editor of *Witness Magazine*. He is an assistant professor of creative writing at the University of the Incarnate Word. He lives in San Antonio with his wife and son.

Jonathan Balcombe is a biologist, author, and a lifelong animal advocate. His 2006 book *Pleasurable Kingdom* is the first in-depth examination of animals' capacity to enjoy life. His subsequent books *Second Nature* and *The Exultant Ark* also present animals in a new light and presage a revolution in the human-animal relationship. His latest book, the *New York Times* bestseller *What a Fish Knows,* explores the private lives of the planet's most misunderstood and exploited vertebrates. Balcombe is director for animal sentience with The Humane Society Institute for Science and Policy, and associate editor for *Animal Sentience*, the first scholarly journal of animal feeling.

ABOUT THE CONTRIBUTORS

Gary Barwin is a writer, composer, and multidisciplinary artist, the author of twenty-one books of poetry and fiction. His national bestselling novel *Yiddish for Pirates* (Random House Canada) was a finalist for both the Governor General's Award for Fiction and the Scotiabank Giller Prize. *No TV for Woodpeckers* (poetry, Wolsak & Wynn) was published in 2017. A finalist for the National Magazine Awards (Poetry), Barwin teaches creative writing at Mohawk College and is currently writer-in-residence at several shelters as well as at McMaster University (2016-2017). He lives in Hamilton, Ontario and at garybarwin.com.

David Brooks, an Australian poet, novelist, short-story writer and essayist, is Honorary Associate Professor at the University of Sydney, where he taught Australian literature from 1991-2013, co-editor of the journal *Southerly*, and the 2015/16 Australia Council Fellow in Fiction. His most recent publications are *Open House* (poetry, 2015), *Napoleon's Roads* (short fiction, 2016), both from the University of Queensland Press, and *Derrida's Breakfast* (Brandl & Schlesinger, 2016), three essays on Derrida and the animal.

Amy Cicchino attended Florida Gulf Coast University and earned an MA in English literature and a BA in English literature with a minor in education. She is a PhD student in rhetoric and communication.

Gabriel Gudding is the author of *Literature for Nonhumans* (Ahsahta, 2015), *Rhode Island Notebook* (Dalkey Archive Press, 2007) and *A Defense of Poetry* (Pitt, 2002). His essays and poems appear in such periodicals as *Harper's Magazine*, *The Nation*, and *Journal of the History of Ideas*, in such anthologies as *Great American Prose Poems*, *Best American Poetry*, *Best American Experimental Writing*, and *&Now: Best Innovative Writing*. His translations from Spanish appear in anthologies such as *The Oxford Book of Latin American Poetry*, *Poems for the Millennium*, and *The Whole Island: Six Decades of Cuban Poetry*.

Diane Josefowicz's short fiction and essays have appeared in *Conjunctions*, *The Saint Ann's Review*, *Fence*, and *Dame*. She holds an MFA in fiction from Columbia University, and a PhD in the history of science from MIT. She lives in Providence, Rhode Island.

Ariana-Sophia Kartsonis has had a number of stories published in anthologies, as well as the journals *Glimmer Train* and *Literal Latte*. She received a "distinguished story" mention in *The Best American Short Stories 2006*. Her first book of poetry, *Intaglio*, winner of the Stan and Tom Wick Prize, was published in 2006 by Kent State University Press. Her second, *The Rub*, winner of the Elixir Editor's Prize, and a chapbook, *Aloha, Vaudeville Doll*, were published in 2014. She is a faculty advisor for *Botticelli Literary/Art Journal* at the Columbus College of Art and Design, where she teaches.

Olga Kotnowska is a freelance creative writer, currently based in Madrid, Spain. She spends most of her time collecting stories, and eventually, when they are ready, transforming them into short stories. In 2010, Olga completed a master of science communication in creative nonfiction writing at

New Zealand's Otago University. She dedicated her dissertation to the notion of using imaginative literature (such as fictional short stories) as a way of (subtly, yet beautifully, through the language of literature) communicating traditionally difficult concepts to the public.

Justin Maxwell's collection of short plays, *A Blinded Horse Dreams of Hippocampi and Other Plays* is just out from Alligator Pear Publishing. He is currently the Daedalus Fellow at Swandive Theatre, where *The Canopic Jar of My Sins* will premier in 2018. He has recently published a play in the literary journal *Eleven Eleven* and essays in *The Fourth River*. His prose has appeared in various journals, including *Contemporary Theatre Review*, *American Theatre Magazine*, *Rain Taxi Review of Books*, *Minnesota History*, and others. He is an assistant professor at the University of New Orleans, where he is an assistant professor in their playwriting MFA.

W.P. Osborn's *Seven Tales and Seven Stories* won the 2013 Unboxed Books Fiction Prize. His short fiction has been in journals such as *Mississippi Review, Another Chicago Magazine, Beloit Fiction Journal, Hotel Amerika, Southern Humanities Review*, and *Gettysburg Review*. He is a professor of English at Grand Valley State University in Allendale, Michigan.

Melanie Rae Thon's most recent books are the novel *The Voice of the River* and *In This Light: New and Selected Stories*. She is also the author of the novels *Sweet Hearts*, *Meteors in August*, and *Iona Moon*, and the story collections *First, Body* and *Girls in the Grass*. Thon's work has been included in *Best American*

Short Stories (1995, 1996), three *Pushcart Prize Anthologies* (2003, 2006, 2008), and *O. Henry Prize Stories* (2006). She is a recipient of a Whiting Writer's Award, two fellowships from the National Endowment for the Arts, the Mountains & Plains Independent Booksellers Association Reading the West Book Award, the Gina Berriault Award, the Utah Book Award, and a writer's residency from the Lannan Foundation. In 2009, she was the Virgil C. Aldrich Fellow at the Tanner Humanities Center. Thon's fiction has been translated into French, Italian, German, Spanish, Croatian, Finnish, Japanese, and Farsi. Originally from Montana, Thon now lives in Salt Lake City, where she teaches in the creative writing and environmental humanities programs at the University of Utah.

J. T. Townley has published in *Harvard Review, Hayden's Ferry Review, Prairie Schooner, The Threepenny Review*, and other magazines and journals. His stories have been nominated for the Pushcart Prize and Best of the Net award. He holds an MFA in creative writing from the University of British Columbia and an MPhil in English from Oxford University, and he teaches at the University of Virginia.

Michael X. Wang received his MFA from Purdue University. He won a 2010 AWP Intro Award in fiction. His work has appeared or is forthcoming in *Glimmertrain, Hayden's Ferry Review*, and *Sycamore Review*.

Laura Madeline Wiseman's essays have appeared or are forthcoming in *Mid-American Review, Sou'wester, Arts & Letters, Southern Indiana Review, The South Loop Review, Pithead

Chapel, Sports Literate, and elsewhere. Her essay "Seven Cities of Good" was an honorable mention in *Pacifica Literary Review*'s 2015 Creative Nonfiction Award. Her essay "Hunger" was selected as the honorable mention by Paul Lipskey for the *Arts & Letters* Susan Atefat Creative Nonfiction Prize. Her newest book is *Velocipede* (Stephen F. Austin University Press, 2016). She teaches at the University of Nebraska-Lincoln.

Kyoko Yoshida was born and raised in Fukuoka, Japan. She studied Oriental history and American literature at Kyoto University, and creative writing at the University of Wisconsin-Milwaukee. She was an honorary fellow at the International Writing Program at the University of Iowa in 2005. Her first collection of short stories in English, *Disorientalism*, was published in 2014 by Vagabond Press. She translates contemporary experimental Japanese poetry and drama. *Spectacle & Pigsty: Poetry by Kiwao Nomura* (Omni-Dawn, 2011, co-translated with Forrest Gander) won the 2012 Best Translated Book Award in Poetry. Her academic fields of interest include contemporary fiction in English and cultural representations of American baseball (*Reading Baseball*, Keio UP, 2014) and its trans-Pacific exchanges in the 1920s and 1930s. She teaches American Literature at Ritsumeikan University.

ABOUT THE EDITOR

A. Marie Houser is an editor, writer, and scholar who has published in the areas of critical animal studies, disability studies, literary theory, and relational psychology. She is a popular presenter who has traveled to Australia, Canada, and Senegal to give talks and lead workshops on writing and editing with a focus on ethics. As an editor, she helped Dr. Melanie Joy's *Why We Love Dogs, Eat Pigs, and Wear Cows: An Introduction to Carnism* become a worldwide phenomenon.

ACKNOWLEDGMENTS

Without contributions, an anthology exists as a terrarium of air: mostly an idea, lovely just to think about. All thanks go to the sixteen writers who brought this anthology into being by sprouting magnificent worlds. Their necessary and moving contributions made the work of the anthology deeply gratifying, as did their enthusiasm and patience.

My gratitude to Nancy and Tom Regan's Culture & Animals Foundation, which provided funding. I dedicate this anthology to the memory of Tom, who wrote *The Case for Animal Rights* in part to buoy the engaged ethics of activism for nonhuman animals. An activist himself, Tom, together with Nancy, established the Foundation to help fund creative and scholarly projects that amplify animal rights-related messages.

Thank you to Martin Rowe, Kara Davis, Wendy Lee, Jasmin Singer, and Mariann Sullivan for the advice and opportunities that gave the project early momentum, and to Kathryn Eddy, Karly Mintz, Okla Elliott (in pace requiescat), and Ryan Scheife of Mayfly Design for help along the way. A special note of appreciation for friends near and far, including contributors Justin Maxwell and Melanie Rae Thon: their correspondence has been a delight.

My most sincere thanks to J.M. Coetzee, whose work is a great and renewing beacon, and whose kindness has been immeasurable.